THE MISFITS

Told by A Behavior Analyst

AUTHOR'S NOTE

The following is based off true events; only the names of
the individuals and institution have been changed.

Dedicated to those who cannot be heard.

Prologue

It was the year 2010. I had just graduated from college, and I had a few years under my belt as one of the managers of a prestigious veterinary hospital. It wasn't bad for a college gig. It also wasn't something I was passionate about, but it paid the bills and the meagre salary felt like a lot at the time, given that I was fresh out of college. That I was actually making more than minimum wage for the first time in my life felt like a miracle. However, I was long overdue for a career transition into something I could really sink my teeth into. It hadn't quite revealed itself, but I knew I was after a job that would change me as much as I would hope to change it. I sat in front of a computer screen and opened an e-mail from a potential employer that read, "You are very persistent." My heart skipped a beat out of anxiety, and I read on to finish the sentence, "but that's a good thing." *Whew*, I thought, *I might be on to something.*

I had just earned a bachelor's degree in Sociology. According to the Florida State University rules, I had fished around one too many times to lock in my major in the psychology field, which is what I really wanted to do. The reason I was so nervous about the e-mail in front of me is because I was given a shot to prove myself to the owner of a behavior analysis (sub-field of psychology) company that had been in business for over 20 years. The owner also happened to be a local psychology guru and a well-known member of the community. Many of her current employees entered through an applied behavior analysis graduate program at Florida State University, and were usually a shoe-in to work for the company long term if they performed well. I, on the other hand, more or less snuck in through the back door. I wasn't prepared to start thinking about going back to school for a graduate degree, and I didn't take my undergrad course work very seriously until the last year or so, when I felt an overwhelming urge to pull my act together and move on with my life. It wasn't that I didn't care about my academic performance; I just woke up every day throughout college at 6:30am, and worked 40 to 50 hours a week, including weekends and holidays, never afforded a true Christmas or Thanksgiving. The trick was performing a balancing act between my academics, a job in management, and my personal life. For that reason, I didn't have an impressive paper trail. I didn't graduate with honors, and I didn't join any clubs outside of the local rugby team. Having not been a distinguished graduate, I also didn't care about any superlatives. I always felt my average academic performance wasn't reflective of my true intelligence or potential. *I just haven't found my niche yet,* I'd say when confronted with less than ideal grades for a semester's worth of work. I was an oddball, a guy off the street trying to dive in with a group of honor roll masters level students. But something in my correspondence with the company owner gave me a chance that I didn't want to waste.

A month after the e-mail correspondence, I got the job, and found myself at Bishop Secondary School, a rehabilitative treatment school, which I'll have the pleasure of discussing throughout this wild story. The ultimate inspiration for this book was the collection of unique personalities I interacted with during my employment there. The first thing one should know about Bishop is that it flew so low under the radar that most people who lived in the same town as the school for 20 plus years never knew it existed. Bishop was a school for children and adolescents who were diagnosed with emotional behavior disorder, conduct disorder, depression, anxiety, oppositional defiance disorder, autism, and many other conditions. While Bishop was structured similar to other schools as far as grades and courses, it had been given a few tweaks. The team of professionals at Bishop consisted of the typical staffing one would expect at a school--principals, teachers, and teaching aides. To supplement the treatment program, however, Bishop used behavior analysts from the company I worked for. We used applied behavior analysis principles and positive behavior support programs to reinforce socially desirable behaviors. Most people will not know what that means. In short, we tried to weed out socially inappropriate behaviors, and replace them with those that are socially acceptable. For someone in my position, this means tirelessly implementing behavior analytic reinforcement procedures, in which students could ascend through level systems that awarded them greater benefits the higher they climbed. The level systems were technical and specific to the school. To paint an accurate picture, students on a higher level status enjoyed more trust from the staff, trust which was then strengthened by that student earning a trip to a community outing to their favorite destination, for example. They could also earn points by means of appropriate behavior, exchanging such points for what was personally meaningful to the student--additional recess time, or extra-one-on one-time with the guitar teacher, for example. The theory being, the higher the level a student is on, the more independent, better-behaved, and trustworthy that student became. The catch was one could only achieve high level status through appropriate behavior. This meant no fighting, no cursing, no leaving campus, no attacking the teacher, no destroying of school property. These were not unreasonable expectations for any school, yet such acts occurred on a daily basis. If a student slipped up and lost his cool, he could be expected to drop a level, and possibly lose privileges.

Bishop was also unique in that its transition program allowed students to rise through the specialized level systems, encouraging the systematic increase of appropriate behaviors while placing greater consequences on inappropriate behaviors, as the expectations of the student increased. This was a perfect model for some students. For example, it allowed many talented student athletes to eventually leave Bishop after rehabilitation and spend their remaining K-12 years in school, playing sports for their preferred high school team, many becoming known for their standout performances. Some students went on to not only become all-star athletes, but to embody qualities that enabled them to become academic and social role models for their peers and the community. A Cinderella story, in which one could turn his life around, and produce meaningful outcomes.

Before the untamed story that was about to unravel came to be, perhaps one of the most exciting components of my new job was that it gave me something extra in common with my father. He began his career in education as a social studies teacher in 1972. Although he would eventually move on to work with the superintendent and represent the teachers union in a number of different ways, teaching was originally where his heart was, distinguishing him as a passionate proponent of the quality of education. I have old black and white photos of him advocating on the streets for parents and educators, surrounded by a mob of similarly-minded hippies as they held up signs to support their cause, protesting against funding cuts for education. To this day, his former students approach him and compliment his teaching methods, lauding him and declaring him, "the coolest teacher I ever had." As a boy I didn't appreciate this, I was always in a hurry. I'd tug on his hand in an effort to pull him away from his nostalgic conversations with people in public (due to his 45 years serving the education industry in some form, he was, and still is, extremely well known and liked by anyone who has anything to do with education). This frequent habit of his former students made eating lunch with him somewhat problematic for me as a child; I was just hungry and didn't want to sit and chat with strange adults. In retrospect I realize how much of an impact he had on so many lives. While my new job wasn't focused strictly on education like his, we shared a common interest in that I brought a particular set of skills into an *education setting*. I worked closely with teachers in the school, collaborating on ideas that culminated in formal behavior programs designed to benefit a particular student. Although, candidly I found myself dropping the behavior analytic approach from time to time. What seemed appropriate in my conversations with discontented, hopeless children, was simply advocating the necessity of education. I couldn't help but taste the irony, as almost my entire life I dodged homework, chased girls, procrastinated, skipped classes in high school to go play music or eat at the Chinese buffet across the street, and was comfortable being an academic underperformer, giving "thank you" cards to my teachers to show my appreciation in hopes to influence a passing grade. Perhaps the latter was an instinctive gesture, foreshadowing my future career in persuading the behavior of others. Nevertheless, there I was preaching about the importance of school. I was hopeful that students would buy in, pull themselves out of their hell, and possibly make a better life for themselves. In retrospect, I probably sounded like the father they never had. But life wasn't that simple at Bishop, it rarely ever is.

At times my efforts would fall victim to heated opposition from the students, who prioritized immediate urges to be violent over the future I envisioned for them. This allowed me to swap unique stories with my father regularly, though it didn't take long for my stories to trump his.

My father recalls teaching in the seventies: "The curriculum was dictated by the state Board of Education and implemented by the local School Board. The scope and sequence of what you taught was state mandated. But in my ten-year teaching experience I had more creative license to present required material than teachers do today." The creative license he speaks of provided an opportunity for teachers to loosely generate their own version of a test to assess how their students were performing. In comparison, the atmosphere of a classroom was vastly different back then. He also recalls playing pranks on the kids with water guns, laughing and learning together, and generally having a good time, while making learning *fun*. Imagine that. He found a method of communication that centered on a good sense of humor. Perhaps that is why he is remembered and revered by his former students. Argumentatively, the seventies was a less fortunate time for children with learning and behavior related challenges. There wasn't exactly an overabundance of acknowledged learning disabilities. People were not casually throwing around terms such as autism, attention deficit hyperactivity disorder (ADHD), or other disorders that impacted learning. In many cases, before the de-institutionalization movement in the 1960s and 1970s, as well as enactment of laws such as Free Appropriate Public Education (FAPE), and the Individuals with Disabilities Education Act (IDEA), a large majority of children on the autism spectrum were placed in institutions; many were thought to be schizophrenic and deemed unteachable from an early age. Surely, characteristics of learning and behavior disabilities were present in the students at the time. There was a general consensus regarding aberrant behavior and how to identify it, which boiled down to the idea that, typically, you know it when you see it. Yet, as was common during this time period, the role of learning pertaining to students with disabilities was not taken seriously. Parents were told by medical professionals to send their kids away to psychiatric residential facilities, and move on with their lives as if their child was just a figment of their imagination. Usually, children with behavior or mental disabilities were met with disciplinary approaches, subjected to corporal punishment, or thrown together in a classroom and forgotten about. There are harrowing accounts of autism spectrum children housed in insane asylums who were experimented on, given LSD, or most reprehensibly, subjected to shock therapy. Such children were poked and prodded by men in white coats with cattle prods to correct behavior. All of these approaches, immoral and deleterious, were closer to hacking at a tree limb rather than striking at the roots.

Thankfully, deplorable stories like these are much less common today. Although we no longer have the man in the white coat carrying his cattle prod, anyone who has come in contact with a child with special needs must ask himself, "Just how far have we come in improving the education of these children?" Though we may not be inflicting direct harm, we are inflicting *indirect* harm through dysfunctional bureaucratic decisions. My experience leads me to believe the answer is not concrete, but rather contingent on several factors;

namely, geography, culture, access to funding, political interest, parent attitudes, and public awareness. In short, one's geography is important as it dictates how progressive the immediately surrounding culture is, indicative of how the local population perceives intellectual disability. There are some regions of the United States where parents are hardly aware of the existence of intellectual disabilities, much less how to access resources to mitigate burdensome circumstances for themselves and their child during his or her educational experience. Depending on the reader, you may or may not be surprised by this. For that matter, I frequently hear accounts from my patients' parents who return from confusing and catastrophic meetings with pediatricians, or local school board members, who dispute evidence that autism is real! This is particularly infuriating and numbing for parents who seek additional supports that may be instrumental in their child overcoming his or her disability, and thereby leading a happier life.

Funding is overtly important, as it determines how salient a special needs program within a school can be. It can also provide supplemental training courses for teachers who work with a special needs child. New research-based approaches to teaching are always evolving in the educational setting. Therefore, in order to retain quality teaching methodologies, such content demands constant visits from professionals in the field, necessitating school funds to do so.

Not surprisingly, political influence plays an integral role in access to special needs education. Those in positions of power, such as principals, superintendents, mayors, senators, and governors, are entrusted with the honorable duty of making life altering decisions for the populace. Such people are emboldened by ability to control public awareness, channels of funding, various streams of revenue, and allocation of materials by either limiting or exposing access to vital information and raw resources. It's no secret that one person in a position of power can alter an outcome to gain personal leverage to serve his interests. In the state of South Carolina, for example, a child with autism can receive funding from Medicaid to receive up to 40 hours a week of behavior analysis therapy. Eight hours of therapy a day for five days a week sounds like a miracle recipe. Imagine if a child had a personal behavior therapist specifically trained in reducing problem behaviors and enhancing communication, following a child around wherever he or she went every day? However, this prescription for therapy is rendered completely useless, as a bylaw exists indicating that none of the funded therapy services shall be allowed in a public, private, or home school. Additionally, many schools in South Carolina have outlawed third party support from people in positions like mine, whose only goal is to support children with special needs and give them a fighting chance. What good reason is there to restrict children's access to professionals who can help them learn? Such bureaucratic stipulations limit a child's availability for behavior therapy to several hours a week--after they leave school, when they are tired, hungry, and overworked. Behavioral intervention is long term therapy, not a quick fix. With such a small window to provide services, it also strains providers who are board certified behavior analysts, as only one child can be seen at a time. This results in extended waiting lists and delayed intervention for families who are desperate, with parents on the verge of a nervous breakdown.

Providers in behavior analysis, who hold master's degrees and achieve national certifications with the behavior analyst certification board, are reported to be equally as effective as what a lawyer can do for a client facing criminal charges, what a psychologist can do to reverse posttraumatic stress disorder, or what an occupational therapist can do to aide someone in overcoming a physical impairment. Congruent with this perception, the Center for Disease Control dedicates several paragraphs on its website to applied behavior analysis, praising the discipline and acknowledging it as a "notable treatment approach," further stating that, "it has become widely accepted among health care professionals." (Center for Disease, 2015 para 9). But such praise for the discipline doesn't always amount to fair treatment. Behavior analysts in the state of South Carolina are offered insulting rates from state funds and insurance companies to do their jobs in rehabilitating children with special needs. This eats away at small businesses, dampens efforts to hire quality therapists, and increases tension on a rope that is already strained. According to the Center for Disease Control's Autism and Developmental Disabilities Monitoring (ADDM) Network, autism was prevalent in 1 in 150 children in the year 2000, and by the year 2012, prevalence rates increased to 1 in 68 children (Center for Disease 2016). It goes without saying, autism is on the rise. Discouragingly, effective early intervention is stymied by all of the red tape from insurance companies and trivial school or state policies, creating a spider web of complications. Parents are left empty handed. Experts aren't allowed to do their jobs. These are people's lives. This is inexcusable.

However, the implications are not limited to only children on the autism spectrum. The United States Surgeon General (1999) concluded, "Thirty years of research demonstrated the efficacy of applied behavioral methods in reducing inappropriate behavior and in increasing communication, learning and appropriate social behavior," (United States Surgeon General, 1999). With the efficacy having been demonstrated and validated by decades of research, it is fortunate to know that the underpinnings and fundamentals of applied behavior analysis do not change from one subject to the next. This allows it to be an interdisciplinary therapy, and therefore, incredibly beneficial for people with intellectual disabilities, emotional behavior disorders, traumatic brain injury, and virtually any and all diagnoses that qualify a student for special education. When it comes to special education, this is an area that would certainly benefit from augmented doses of reinforcement from experts who are specially trained in working with disabled populations. Special education teachers are often overwhelmed. They themselves are desperately seeking help from anyone willing to lend a hand. I've had many conversations with educators who wish they could receive more training, more support in their classroom, and tell me in confidence that when they solicited help from their administration, they were met with a cold shoulder. Even in small education classrooms, one child with moderate behavior problems can easily feel like two. As my father would say, "Teachers are generally under-appreciated and over worked. But good teachers love to teach." Teachers *want* to do better. Providers *want* in. So what's the problem? The political agenda.

For hypothetical purposes, let us imagine that a given elementary school receives $11,000 from the state per enrolled student. Let us further imagine that this school boasts a student population of 800 students. For all intents and purposes, the school has received $8,800,000 in funding that shall be applied to any and all means necessary for the purposes of education. Where the public falls short is in our ability to track such funds and how they are utilized. I've sat in school-related meetings on behalf of my clients whose disability mandates that a non-verbal child receive assistive technology to have means of communication, or perhaps an additional staff member in the classroom to meet the child's intense behavior needs. Often I am told that such resources are not available for the student. This can be a violation of the IDEA law, which entitles disabled students to such means to facilitate their communication and gain independence. When I ask questions about where funding is going on behalf of the student, and why it seems inaccessible, there seems to be mass confusion, school representatives tend to clam up, and I'm met with disapproving "How dare you!" facial expressions. These are taxpayer's dollars from income state taxes and property taxes that mysteriously disappear before our eyes.

Broadly speaking, "the US is tied with Switzerland for the top spot in per-capita student expenditure," and sports "over $12,000 on average being spent per student per year for education." (the U.S. is tied n.d.). The gravity of such expenditures doesn't truly sink in until we start asking the right questions, such as, "Is our money well spent?"; "Does it produce quality outcomes?" Astonishingly, when compared with other countries, the "U.S. public schools lag behind in basic mathematics, reading and science, despite such huge expenses on public education." (the U.S. n.d.) In the District of Columbia, where per capita spending reaches the highest across the United States, at a whopping $29,349 per student, between the years 2010 and 2011, "83 percent of the eighth graders in these schools were not "proficient" in reading and 81 percent were not "proficient" in math." (Jeffrey T. 2014 para 1). The educational outcome is far from justifying the financial means. Tracing a paper trail that specifies where taxpayer's money goes once it hits the school bank account is made nearly impossible. Incontrovertibly, it appears resoundingly clear that spending more money does not equate to better education. Quite plausibly, spending money smarter would certainly be more productive. More transparent tracking of capital will hold schools accountable, ensuring that the funds are being used as intended. Far too often, a special needs child is left empty handed because of a misappropriation of money, which, not surprisingly, boils down to politics, and whomever has the ultimate oversight of spending. If school superintendents are cruising their yachts in the mid-Atlantic, but their schools can't rub together two pennies to purchase printing paper, then we have a fairly serious problem on our hands.

The unfortunate reality is that rather than spending time working with a team of educational professionals discussing various methods to help a special needs student improve his learning ability, much of my time is exhausted by trying to convince these very professionals that it is *important* for this student to learn. We should not cast aside a child simply because it takes more effort to get through to him. Certainly I am not out to smear or besmirch the reputation of schools that are doing the right thing and serving our children appropriately and passionately. In fact, I have seen some schools go above and beyond to help children with their special needs, and I have been happy to consult with them and be a part of their team. In one unique, incredibly moving case, I once came across a group of teachers who came together and raised money to donate to an intellectually delayed student whose family was living in the backseat of a car, because the mother couldn't afford a deposit on a rental house. It is wonderful to see teachers form lasting impressions with children and periodically check in on them throughout their life. As previously mentioned, the culture of a school, it's attitude towards those with special needs, funding availability, and politics all play an essential role in how well any child with special needs will perform both behaviorally and academically if given the opportunity. However, parents need to feel empowered to self-advocate, and we simply can't expect common sense to prevail. I always encourage my patients' families to challenge school personnel when they refuse to compromise. Ask questions such as, "Where do the funds go that are allotted on behalf of my child?"; "If I am unhappy with the school's ability to teach my child, where do the funds go when I disenroll my child and place him in another school?"; "How do I ensure that my child is being offered the best education accessible in our area, with the latest technology upgrades affordable?"; "Can you have someone perform a functional behavior assessment to determine the root of my child's problem behavior rather than repetitively suspending him or threatening expulsion?"

From my experience, I've found that early intervention is the key to success. This theory is solidified by years of research. The human brain is constantly pruning itself; activity is particularly high-pitched between childhood and puberty, producing information necessary to function, while trying to rid itself of extraneous details. The brain instructs the body to behave in certain ways that are reinforced by one's interaction with the environment. With each repetition of behavior that results in a favorable outcome for the individual, such behavior is strengthened, leading that person to repeat that behavior again in the future as a means to access his or her wants and needs.

Therefore, a child's ability to learn new skills, particularly those as complex as language and socialization, is greatly diminished with age. It baffles me when state legislators don't take early intervention seriously. Consequently, the governing bodies that neglect the research end up fronting the bill, along with taxpayers in the long run. When a disabled child is no longer at an age where he can be formally educated, he either becomes financially dependent on his family, or the state he lives in. As cold as it sounds, if politicians and legislators only deal in numbers, they should consider the following: With heavy hitting intervention strategies from an early age, children with disabilities have a fighting chance to eventually get a job and become a contributing member of society, as opposed to a financial burden to the state many years later.

One facet of my job is to perform as a behavioral consultant in special education classrooms. Put simply, when a child with special needs proves to be exceedingly difficult for a teacher, I am called in on behalf of the school to form a behaviorally analytic opinion on the child's challenging behaviors, using objective data and graphs. Aside from the child's own functions that may lead him or her to behave in a particular pattern, what is also under the microscope is the teacher's approach to the child. Perhaps the most disheartening event I encounter is a teacher who still teaches from behind her desk. We are currently in an age with an explosion of technology. I have seen non-verbal autistic children who will bite, scratch, and tantrum for two hours straight, work I-phones, I-pads, and computers better than their adult counterparts. Such devices are even used to replace vocal communication for children with cognitive deficits who cannot speak, but may be able to manipulate buttons and respond to pictures on a screen, thereby giving them a voice. There is an outworn method of teaching, in which one expects a toddler with a dual diagnosis of autism and ADHD to sit on the floor "crisscross-applesauce" while the teacher sits in a chair and reads a book for twenty minutes. If the toddler acts out, the teacher instinctively places him in time out. After all, she recalls this being a consequence she herself would have received as a young girl who was misbehaving. While time outs can be effective when used strategically, this may not be the appropriate solution. In my experience, the disabled toddler usually can't handle time-out because he doesn't cognitively grasp the concept, or doesn't retain the physiological means to sit still, which is what landed him in time-out in the first place. Before you know it, the toddler is breakdancing on the carpet, running on top of chairs and desks, and bouncing the basketball off the teacher's head. Moreover, all of this activity is much more fun and reinforcing than having to sit still! As honorable as a teacher's intentions may be, this method is antiquated and serves no functional purpose.

So where are the kinks? Believe it or not, the situation described above is pervasive in educational and recreational settings. This can be a problem, because a distracted administration may ignore special education classrooms in lieu of actions that garner the school more public approval. One must remember that special education children are the *minority* in most public schools, the actions of the parents with children who make up the other 90% or so of the student population serve a different agenda. This is also a public awareness problem, because there is a general concept among parents and teachers that punishing behaviors corrects the behaviors long-term (more time-outs, more spanking, etc.). It is a funding and training problem because the teacher clearly isn't prepared to adjust her curriculum or teaching style to fit the learning needs of the child. And it is a political problem; either the parent demands the school fix her child, or the school demands the parent improve her parenting skills (I am usually caught somewhere in between).

While Bishop School isn't perfect, what set it apart from the antiquated methods was its long strides to counter this punitive, divisive approach, and to work collectively with a similar mindset to achieve common goals, as opposed to having political interference from parties vying for competing interests. In retrospect, there wasn't much funding being channeled into the school at the time, so there were no finances to argue about, aside from the fact that the school was broke. Scientific experiments and research are not conducted at Bishop, yet those who believed in what I personally perceive as the Bishop mission, "To understand, and treat behavior problems within the students, as opposed to simply mismanaging them," found solace in this refreshing and steadfast approach.

Bishop School is a place that impacted me greatly, and shaped many professional decisions I make today with my client caseload as a master level certified behavior analyst. What I found interesting during the years after I left Bishop, was how my experiences there widened my scope of the world. The realization of how I positively benefitted from these experiences crept up on me over time, slowly tugging at me. Subconscious memories I had safely tucked away became conscious points of reference for navigating a professional career filled with daily conflict. The realization was something like a cool, soft sheet, slowly being removed from my face. It was undoubtedly the most intense time of my career to date, which may be why I needed several years away from Bishop to understand the importance of what I had endured. I am forever thankful for the experience. From day one I was injected with a high dose of shock and utter disbelief at the things I would witness. Within the first hour, I watched a student wrestled to the ground by a police officer, who then handcuffed him and zip-tied his legs together before placing him in the back of his police cruiser, so the student wouldn't kick the windows out. From that point on, I knew that if I could survive Bishop, I could survive anything in the professional world of behavior analysis.

Moving forward, one must know how rampant and pervasive child abuse cases were with the students at Bishop. This was never clearer to me than when I learned that any children who were victims of abuse, who were under the care of the Department of Children and Families, were not allowed to have their pictures taken and shown publicly. This was done in order to protect them from their perpetrators who may seek them out and wish to cause them harm again. Sadly, this explained why I opened up the Bishop yearbook and found that almost half the students' pictures were missing.

Poverty-stricken, hungry, unhealthy, unhygienic, and ill-tempered, the students' emotions were extraordinary. They fought, cried, screamed, cursed, spit, kicked, and ran; loved, hugged, laughed, failed, and succeeded all over again. One can't stand by and watch events at Bishop without being moved, for better or for worse. The students' responses to everyday stressors were overpowering; they forced me to feel what they were feeling. Their visceral, potent reactions to everyday events illustrated a representation of how raw and agonizing their lives came to be, appealing to my generosity but always testing the limits of my patience.

Chapter 1

Breakfast Blues

A clamorous shrieking sound similar to squeaky car brakes was triggered as the bus doors grudgingly peeled open. An odious, resentful stench emanated from within, as if a crack had formed in the earth and the world's best kept acrid smell was being released. The bus driver was impatiently glaring down at me from her position in the driver's seat, the height of which supported her air of superiority. Her hair was black and frizzy, she sported a plain white T-shirt with holes, and she was overweight to the extent that, upon taking the driver's seat, the steering wheel became cushioned onto her stomach, effectively lodging her in place.

A thick, southern accent pierced the air. "Best hurry up and get these kids of the bus now you hear?" she said, as she discharged her latest swell of tobacco spit into her cup. Now I knew what was contributing to the stench on the bus. I flirted with the idea of a sycophantic bow. "At your service, my liege," I began to say, but then, remembering my manners, I replied, "You're a little early, we don't usually unload for another five minutes."

"Ya'll complain 'bout me being late, then you stand here and complain about's me being early. Which one you want? Choose." Deputy Richards trailed closely behind me, laughing at my misfortune.

"Well, I wasn't exactly complaining, more or less stating a fact. Go ahead and send them out," I say. The grumpy driver waved her hands signaling for the kids to depart the bus, and began mumbling something under her breath, likely taking issue with me for something I had no control over. I never understood how we got off on the wrong foot, given the 60 seconds a day we had to interact, but she tended to dislike everyone, so I didn't take it personally.

The first student off the bus was one who I would come to know quite well during my time at Bishop. A damaged child with tricks up his sleeves at every turn.

"Good morning, Chad," I said.

"Fuck you!" he snapped in response.

I sighed. *The pleasant sounds of my morning routine. Another insult I'll let roll off my shoulder,* I said to myself. There were no preliminaries with Chad, he liked to jump right in. In my left hand I hastily tightened the grip on the black and yellow metal detector that measured approximately a foot and a half long, my right hand delicately balancing my coffee mug. I loved that mug, it was all white with red italicized writing that read, "Behavior Counts." Scanning the students for weapons wasn't in the job description. Chad looked a mess as usual. He stood with one hand supporting his beltless jean shorts, the other hand occupied by his mouth, as he returned to sucking his thumb. His oversized white T-shirt blew in the wind while he struggled to keep his feet inside his shoes, which were lacking laces as usual. I scanned the metal detector along the outline of his small body from head to toe. No beeps. Chad was not carrying any potential weapons today.

"Don't even try me today, Deputy!" said Chad as he turned towards us both and raised his two middle fingers.

I exchanged a look with the menacing Deputy Richards who stood next to me drinking his protein shake. "How ya like that," I said. "He's sharing, one middle finger for you and one for me." The deputy grabbed Chad by the shoulder with one hand like someone would grab a misbehaving kitten, and stabilized him so he couldn't run away.

"What do you want me to do with him Clark? Little boy like this, can't have him out here ripping and running, coming off the bus cursing at adults, especially the law. I know that's a common thing around here, but I all be damned if *I* get used to it."

"Hold on to him for just a minute while I get the rest of these kids off the bus," I replied, appreciatively, yet wary of Deputy Richard's temper.

"Hi Mr. Clark!" Trevor met my gaze, his astronaut sneakers judged the gap from the last step on the bus to the ground below, as he clumsily closed the distance. While he managed to stick the landing, Trevor's cumbersome backpack full of toys weighed his frail shoulders down so heavily that he fell backwards onto the steps. Close behind him, Eddie, appeared, half asleep, with dry syrup on his chin. He laughed and stumbled off the bus while trying to step over Trevor. Shortly after, a head emerged from inside the bus with an arm coiled aggressively around it. It would appear that Zack found himself in one of Cole's headlocks again.

"Man ya'll quit playin! I want my breakfast!" boomed a voice that rebounded off the bus windows. Jacob parted the two entangled boys and moved between them to the front of the line as he exited the bus. A few more stragglers casually filed off the bus and formed a line in front of me. Duncan was among them, forever distinguished by his blazing red hair. Duncan, fond of self-talk, often failed to engage the attention of a specific listener, and usually ended up talking to himself in his own, quirky way. As if to illustrate this point, I heard him ask, "Is the internet working today?" His voice just above a whisper, addressing no one in particular and glancing around nervously, his eyes jumping from the ground to the sky, and back again. Grant jumped through the air, using the last step of the bus as his platform for takeoff. Upon landing, he planted his feet in a wide stance, and played a spirited air guitar solo to accompany the music playing in his ears. The music, oddly enough, was delivered by a pair of headphones that extended down to a mid-1990s cd player encased in a fanny pack fastened around his waist. "Brian Jones, who helped found Rolling Stones, could play over 60 instruments!"

"Thank you for that fact, Grant."

I flipped the switch of the metal detector back to the "on" position to continue scanning each student for weapons. But before I could take my first step to begin, I heard, "Oh Mr. Clark... don't forget about me!" Zahra jumped off the bus, flaunting her imitation diamonds on her shirt. Never one to be shy, she began twirling in circles as if she was modeling for a nearby camera crew. She appreciated a flare for the dramatic entrances, deserving of her own reality show.

"Glad you are feeling so spritely this morning, Zahra, dance yourself into line."

One by one, I scanned each student with the metal detector, allowing them to proceed to the breakfast area, but not before giving the following directions as if I had recited the speech from memory; "Trevor you are clear to go but lose the Star Wars Chewbacca mask; Eddie pull up your pants, we don't need to see your underwear, and if you aren't saving that syrup on your chin for later, go ahead and wipe it off. Zack and Cole, no rough housing on the bus, and preferably no rough housing at all because one of you inevitably ends up losing your temper, and neither of you can afford suspensions or to have your nose broken again. Jacob, you have been doing a great job lately so keep up the good work, remember if you get frustrated with work you have to ask to leave the room *before* you get out of control, or ask to talk to Mr. Morales or myself. Grant, I will be seeing you today, hopefully during your guitar class, but you have to keep those headphones out of your ears during class or our deal is off. Zahra, glad you decided to actually come to school today; remember you have visiting hours with Mrs. Rehder and your son so stay out of trouble. Let's all have a great, productive day!" My coffee was starting to kick in.

Some students nodded in agreement, some of them feigned as if they were listening, but they all made their way down to breakfast and resumed their normal morning banter. I glanced back over at Chad, who was still under the deputy's control, yet wriggling and wrestling to break free like a squirrel caught in a snare trap. Chad shot daggers out of his eyes, "Turn me loose dammit!"

The deputy stood unamused. "Chad, I'm gonna make somebody famous today, don't let it be you," the Deputy replied casually. That was his favorite line.

While the relief of Chad not carrying weapons settled in, he delivered his usual dose of verbal venom by using profanity towards me immediately after exiting the school bus. Per his behavior program, there were consequences for this action.

"Alright Chad, you cursed out an adult, you know what you have to do. You need to go to building 15 to cool off, then go to class and turn your day around."

Chad resolved to hold still, and took a deep breath as if reconciling with himself. "Ok," he said. "I'll go. I'll walk to building 15 by myself. I'm sorry."

Relieved, I told Chad, "You made a good decision just now. I'm proud of you." As the deputy released Chad from his authoritative grip, Chad took no more than five steps before screaming, "I don't care bitch! Can't make me go anywhere! Suck my dick!"

This was not the vernacular that most people expect when interacting with a seven year old. Chad was just a child, a seven year old going on eighteen. As usual, Chad ignored my instructions and ran behind a building, losing both shoes along the way, the bottom of his feet covered in black dirt.

At least this time he didn't throw his shoes on the classroom roof just to spite me.

More than likely, I would need backup to corral Chad in a building where he would not disrupt campus. I reached for the radio wire wrapped around my ear and held the talk button down on the port attached to my belt. Doing so allowed me to communicate with campus staff, who also wore walkie talkie head pieces, "Chad has a verbal aggression and is refusing to go to building 15," I announced routinely, with the smoothness of a disc jockey speaking to his audience, letting them know what songs were coming up over the next hour.

Throughout the eight hour day, I would go on to make hundreds of calls over the radio similar to this one. Inevitably, as soon as Chad began behaving appropriately, there would be a similar issue with another student that would need to be addressed safely and effectively. I, or another team member was sure to put out a call on average of every four to five minutes regarding any one of the distressed children or adolescents who made up our student population.

"Mark is running away from campus." "Roger has threatened to bring a bomb to school tomorrow." "I need assistance in building 7, Johnny is destroying the room and throwing a chair at the teacher," "Can someone please pull Heather out of class and speak with her? She is threatening to kill herself," "Chris has taken his clothes off again and is dancing on the table." "Fight in building 18, I need IMMEDIATE ASSISTANCE!"

This was all in a day's work at Bishop Secondary School. As a behavior analyst I was in the thick of it all. It was a lot like trying to put out a forest fire; as soon as some flames are contained, another area requires 1200 gallons of water per minute to contain the growing hazard. Sometimes I felt like I was running in circles aimlessly.

This particular day was no different, I circled the campus looking for Chad, who ran barefoot around the school, all the while taunting those in his path, hurling insult after insult. Periodically, I would dodge a rock thrown at my head. I would often engage in internal dialogue during these moments, *"I am a grown man chasing a child as he mocks me and throws rocks at my head, is this what my life has come to? I need to be careful running because if I trip and fall flat on my face, the other kids will laugh at me. Wait, I have a college degree, I shouldn't be worrying about getting bullied anymore…right?"*

When I caught him, I would safely escort him to building 15, sometimes called "the chill room." The chill room was an idea suggested by my supervisor at the time, and fellow behavior analyst, Mr. Morales. Its intended use was to serve as a neutral environment where the students would be taken until they were considered "de-escalated"; that is, the student is under instructional control, no longer displaying maladaptive behaviors, and can safely return to class.

40

I can't lie. Bishop Secondary was uncouth. Instead of fancy classrooms with the latest technology in which every child was awarded his or her own I-pad or computer screen, students and teaching staff were subjected to red clay colored portable buildings with ineffective air conditioning units. Temperatures would climb to the upper 90s, and we would sweat through our day, most of us instituting our own closed-toe shoe policy (one has to be mindful of his toes being broken by the students during a behavior meltdown). The city workers were always late mowing the grass. Our school sign was so faded it looked as if it had been salvaged from a junkyard. There weren't many parking spots, so our staff would create our own parking in undesignated areas, where we were sure to open our car doors and step in an ant hill. And sometimes it was so hot we would pray for rain because, unlike other schools where the students simply used the rain shelter, when it rained at Bishop Secondary, you simply got wet.

Yet everything that made Bishop such a startling counterculture territory is also what made it a unique opportunity. Where else can a child go to receive education where you can curse out a teacher, break a window, step outside for a few minutes to cool off, and finish your day answering questions from a story? Bishop is a rehabilitative treatment school for children with intellectual disabilities, often accompanied by emotional behavior disorders (EBD), autism, and a number of other diagnoses. During my time at Bishop we maintained a student population of approximately 70-80 students from first grade through high school. That's approximately 1-2% of the 40,000 kindergarten through twelfth grade student population in the county at the time. We had our own graduation program, as well as a transition program that allowed students to mainstream into "regular" schools if their behavior improved over the course of therapy. Our students were sent to us by the school system because they had a track record that plagued their educational history. This meant that traditional schools rejected the student's enrollment as soon as they saw the words "conduct disorder" on their file, or students were expelled due to being unteachable and aggressive or destructive. Bishop students simply could not be contained in a regular school, and Bishop staff were their last hope before the student ended up in a state wide inpatient psychiatric program, incarcerated, or worse.

The irony of our program is that it became so reinforcing that some of the students who were eligible to leave, actually chose to stay at Bishop due to some of the flexibilities they were provided. For reasons transparent, they found it difficult to leave such a reinforcing, supportive, positive atmosphere. The staff were consummate professionals who underwent the daily work stress of being aggressed upon and cursed at, something that could not be asked of teachers at mainstream schools. The students did not have to earn respect; respect was an endless resource afforded to them by staff. Sure there were consequences to students' poor decisions. But after being kicked, hit, and punched, our staff would then turn around and offer support, love, and instruction--no grudges held. I couldn't say the same about any other place in the world.

For most Bishop students with special needs, this model of education propelled them forward. Their individualized education was cushioned daily with social skills training emphasizing communication and problem solving

43

techniques that wouldn't have been offered elsewhere. Some of the students that attended Bishop went home at the end of the day without certainty as to whether they would have dinner that night, and they came back the next day because they were guaranteed at least two square meals by the public education system. Like other schools, academics were important at Bishop, yet we cared more about the well-being of our students than earning straight A's.

It would be dishonest to behave as if all Bishop students received gratification and happiness through this system. A small percentage of students would slip through the cracks, the permanent damage done before they ever arrived at the school. In addition to their accompanying diagnosis, many students carried a chip on their shoulder. Some were chronically leery from having been emotionally and physically abused; some came from homes where they were sexually assaulted, beaten, raped, neglected, and told all their life that they were worthless. Some had files as thick as a telephone book detailing, for example, how they watched their father murder their mother and then hang himself, leaving the child to starve to death. I recall one instance in which our school resource officer confiscated a YouTube video that he shared with me. In the video, a young boy was surrounded by adults with whom he was seemingly familiar with, judging by the video participants' body language. I watched this boy enter a freestyle rap battle with adults three times older than him. Marijuana smoke filled their lungs and eclipsed the computer screen, gun handles could be seen from the waistline of the video participants who waved their gang signs, while gang related rap songs ensued that covered topics from shooting police officers to having sex with prostitutes. When the amateur videographer panned over to the child rapping between his own puffs of marijuana, I immediately recognized the child as a Bishop student who I worked with every day--he was eight years old. During my time at Bishop, this student repeatedly was in and out of the school, his desk often vacated at times when he was in the juvenile detention center.

Chad was now disrupting the entire campus, and more staff were needed to corral him to building 15. Chad knew the perfect recipe for chaos, and he was a master manipulator. When Chad was in a bad mood, he developed a hankering to agitate anyone and everyone who crossed his path. There are many students who walked the Bishop campus with reactivity problems similar to that of a hairpin trigger; it didn't take much to set them off. Any minute now Chad would approach one of his targets (usually someone twice his age and size), and gleefully tell them to "Fuck off." He was pulling the strings. Chad had also learned by now that he could absolutely trust someone like me to protect him from others as much as I would protect him from himself.

Just ahead, Chad swaggered towards a brooding Jacob, forever the disgruntled tenth grader, who resembled the cartoon character "Sylvester the Cat." School breakfast now in hand, Jacob cared not that the grits on his Styrofoam plate had overflowed and begun to trickle down his hand. His red and black striped shirt was half untucked; he walked with both feet pointing outwards at 45 degree angles, as if they had been secretly magnetized and were constantly trying to achieve a hard 90 degree right angle. To make matters worse, Jacob was a hot head; he wore an indignant facial expression that indicated at some point in his life he had been insulted and his face had been frozen in time. Not unlike most students at Bishop, he was known for aggressively overreacting.

Chad began mouthing off unintelligible utterances to Jacob, and my brain started working double time.

Why did I wear these shoes today? I can't move fast enough. Okay, think preventative, disarm the bomb before it goes off.

As I scurried through the unmowed grass I said, "Jacob, don't listen to him just continue walking, I'll be sure to award you pro-social points for your program." I was trying to squeeze in a little guidance before Chad found just the right buttons to push, igniting the firestorm soon to erupt within Jacob. Jacob paused long enough to consider what I said, as if there was a fly buzzing around his head and he was considering whether or not to swat at it. He picked up his toast from his breakfast plate and casually tasted it, putting the corner of the bread in his mouth, then looked at Chad expectantly.

Please don't say anything Chad. I really hope Jacob is in a good mood today. Why don't they mow this grass? I pondered.

There was no transparent explanation for why Chad challenged everyone that crossed his path, except that he fed off of negative energy. Inside, Chad was miserable, and he loved making others miserable too. I was still moving quickly towards the two, acknowledging the following two facts to be true when tested 100% of the time. First, Chad has always demonstrated an incapacity to discern whether or not he is outmatched. Second, Jacob always failed to differentiate a real threat from a perceived one, the fact that Chad was half his age and size wouldn't slow him down.

I was closer now, but still unable to pick up on exactly what Chad was saying. To my surprise and relief, Jacob reluctantly began to step away from Chad, choosing to ignore what was said. *It's a miracle.* I thought to myself. *I'll take the small victory.* Jacob continued to increase his distance from Chad, and I thought maybe my preventative effort had been effective; or, perhaps Jacob's pride was still hurt from several days prior, when

I tackled him just before he smashed a poorly placed 2 x 4 across a student's head outside of his classroom. Jacob turned away from Chad and gave him the cold shoulder. The situation might have unfolded differently had Jacob not been preoccupied with his breakfast. He continued to enjoy his bread, which he chewed methodically, experimenting with its flavors as he dipped it into the pile of grits on his plate. Unflinchingly, Chad persisted, and I was close enough now to hear the insults, "Jacob…You're a piece of shit dummy faced cracker!" Jacob froze. The bread fell several inches from his mouth to the plate with a splat. With Chad distracted, I maneuvered myself close enough to be within reach of him and took him assertively by the arm, hoping I could position him far enough away before Jacob buried his fist in Chad's face.

The moment was tense. Chad might as well have been a matador, waving a red muleta at Jacob, inviting an attack, pressing the buttons; he knew exactly how to get a rise out of someone. *Please don't say anything else Chad, I* thought again. *If I could just move him far enough away then this will be over quickly.* "Jacob, you're so ugly your

49

momma didn't want you so she threw you away!" shouted
Chad. Shockingly, a second miracle repeated itself as
Jacob showed unparalleled restraint, his eyes crossed,
yet his bread and grits found the path to his mouth again,
and though his shoulders tensed, his feet still pointed
outwards, he wasn't willing to stoop to Chad's level. He
had matured, or so I thought. I had just begun to feel
comforted that the situation didn't escalate further. And
then it happened.

"Jacob, your momma is a fat fucking bitch and she sucks
dicks in jail!" screamed Chad.

Seconds passed. My face was stinging. The bull had
attacked, there was a flurry of commotion, an eruption of
profanity and screams that could be heard a mile away.
Why was my face stinging? Everything happened so fast.
I was wearing the buttered, watery grits on my shirt that
were originally running down Jacob's hand. I noted the
Styrofoam plate on the ground next to my shoe, *Why
would they serve cornbread at breakfast?* Processing
what had passed, I gathered that I had snatched Chad's
arm just in time to physically hurl him out of the path of
Jacob's left hook, I had become rather skilled at

redirecting flying fists, though not skilled enough. I turned around and received a torpedo of a slap in the face from a now turbulent Chad, who was not thankful whatsoever for my involvement. Suppressing my anger, I stood above Chad, hunched my back over the top of his head, folded him up in my arms and covered as much of his body as I could with my own. My back absorbed most of the punishment from Jacob's fists as they were aimed at Chad with the intent of knocking his head off his shoulders. Chad continued to be obstreperous, eager to fight back against someone twice his size and age. "I'm going to rip your eyeballs out!" screamed Jacob, wholeheartedly determined to do just that. He pulled at my hair, trying to pry me away from Chad, knowing he only had seconds to inflict maximum damage before time would run out.

Other campus staff and fellow behavior analysts came to my aid, physically restraining Jacob and subsequently verbally de-escalating him after he ran around campus for twenty minutes smashing everything in his path. Other students walked to their classrooms and passively watched Jacob put on a show much to their own amusement. He was a personal favorite amongst the students to watch when angry. They laughed at his strange, immature behavior of punching steel doors or head butting walls, trying to show how tough he was, often resulting in a silly injury to himself. He had been known to commit overly impulsive, rage filled attempts to prove his strength, and time and time again he would come up short. Once, during a behavior meltdown, he thought he could karate chop down a tree with his hand, but he just shattered his bones and ended up in a cast. Though he lacked rational foresight, and regularly overestimated his own strength, he at least seemed to learn from experience. At some point, Jacob would be requested to calm down or he would be put in handcuffs and possibly arrested; he would eventually comply, without further injury.

I was now participating in a two person escort with Mr. Morales. One responsible adult on each side of Chad, I carefully under hooked Chad's arm and walked him to building 15. Chad was laughing at me,

"Mr. Clark you're stupid and smelly!"

I'm not stupid, but I am smelly now, I thought.

Chad was thrilled with his handy work, and he was just getting started. I was angry. But the first thing you learn at Bishop is never to demonstrate frustration in front of a student. Do this, and they will eat you alive. Grits dripped from my shirt, my face was red, my back was swelling up from Jacob's fists, I didn't know where my coffee was. It wasn't even 9:15 am yet.

Chapter 2

The Candy Bar Conundrum

I can never find the right key, I thought. Chad was still hurling inventive insults in my ear and sweat was dripping down my eyes. The door to building 15, affectionately known as the chill room, had to stay locked so that we could always account for students when they absconded from the classroom. My shins were getting blasted by Chad's feet as he repeatedly donkey kicked me in an attempt to free himself from my grip and wreak more havoc across campus. It was somewhat like trying to contain a tethered horse desperately wanting to snap his rope; meanwhile doing the opposite of what your instincts tell you by remaining completely disciplined and non-reactive. In these moments the sense of urgency to get the door open cannot be overstated. "I can't find my key!"

Mr. Morales, ever the team player, would pinpoint the right key on his own key ring while I began to solely focus on restraining Chad, which would buy us just the four to six seconds we needed to finally unlock the door. Inside we would safely release Chad into the room in hopes of a brief respite.

"Mr. Clark, haven't you learned by now how to use a fork when you eat your breakfast?" joked Mr. Morales as he noted the grits on my shirt. His school key chain looped onto a short, yellow, nylon string that he spun around his fingers out of habit while he talked.

Laughter was always the best remedy for high intensity situations. If I had to be stuck in building 15 for the next four hours, Mr. Morales was the best staff to accompany me. The grits on my shirt no longer bothered me enough to be grumpy about it. If it did, I would have turned in my two week notice back when I was covered in spit, milk, dirt, fruit punch, water, glue, coca cola, bleach, cake, pie, and especially that one time when one of the students urinated in a cup and threw it at me.

"I really find it more fun to eat with my fingers," I retorted.

My eyes scanned the room. Experience is the best teacher. We had learned by now the advantages of less clutter. This meant fewer opportunities for students to hurl harmful objects at us. However, creativity still rules the day. For some students, their shoes acted as a convenient prop for a 50 mph fast ball. There was a heavy brown desk and brown chair that stared at us ominously from the far corner of the room. I thought about the time we moved that furniture into this room and I strained myself wriggling it awkwardly through the doorway. I remembered thinking how ugly it was; judging by our culture's modern ability to make things lighter and smaller, I had guessed that the desk and chair were at least thirty years old. The weight of the chair and desk was no coincidence; these particular pieces had been selected because they were too cumbersome for the elementary-age students to pick up and use as a weapon, though there were scratches and dents on every corner from the thousands of times that very behavior had been attempted. At best, the kids would tip the desk over, but once it was down, they couldn't set it upright again.

The walls were freshly painted by some of the older, more willing students a month before. It was a win-win for both staff and students. We needed the room to be painted in a way that was a little more uplifting than the blank grey canvas that existed before, and the students wanted to avoid classwork. What once was a nondescript and unremarkable grey colored wall, was now decorated with a mural that illustrated green trees, birds, traffic lights, and was sprinkled with little hints of painted magic from the students experimenting with their own artistic creativity. Truthfully, the work was sloppy and amateur at best, but a step in the right direction, and their effort was noble.

I fiddled with my keys yet again, opening the closet door to retrieve a clipboard with a documentation sheet on it. If a student was brought here, all time spent in the building had to be logged. Information such as who the student is, which staff were present, and duration of behavior episode were all relevant to quality assurance auditors. What made documentation difficult was the probability that staff wouldn't have a free hand to write with. Irate students are not willingly walking into the chill room with a smile on their face, but just as in Chad's case, are rather dragged into the room kicking and screaming. This building is a safety precaution in the event students want to hurt themselves or someone else. Once inside, students may continue their fury by slamming their own head on the walls, clawing at my face, punching, biting, pulling the fire alarm, or spraying staff with the fire extinguisher, among other things. Needless to say, documentation on the clipboard is a tall order, and one is hard pressed to make it accurate. But for the moment my hands were free, so I moved to quickly take advantage of my time, which would surely come to an end any second. Upon opening the closet, I see miscellaneous toiletry items such as paper towels, extra toilet paper, several brooms, a small brown belt for a child, a yellow mop bucket and mop handle, as well as cleaning products such as bleach, rubber gloves, and all-purpose surface cleaner. Strangely enough, all these items can trigger memories from minutes, hours, or days past. The bleach, for example, has been thrown on me before, and several students have tried to drink it in an act of self-loathing defiance. The mop has been used to clean the floors when students intentionally defecated or urinated outside of the bathroom, sometimes playing in their excrement or throwing it at staff during their manic depressive state. And the belt was taken from a ten-year-old student who locked himself in the bathroom and tried to hang himself before watchful staff interrupted him. As I hurriedly moved the pen across the paper, logging the date and time, I finally noticed a silver, metal baseball bat with a black handle laying upside down against the wall.

Hardship can bring people together. When you spend enough time with someone experiencing situations of extremely high stress day in and day out, you begin to form a bond with that person. Undoubtedly, the repeated exposure to thousands upon thousands of high intensity crises carved the path for Mr. Morales and I to acknowledge one another's value, which strengthened through our non-verbal communication. Mr. Morales taught me about strategy, such that one can't always meet opposition by steamrolling a child and telling him it's "my way or nothing at all." As a behavior analyst, he developed an efficient method of giving the child choices, letting him feel in control so he is much more likely to take ownership of his decision. I knew at times when he raised his voice to someone like Cole, for example, that he wasn't incentivizing Cole to lash out, but instead was aiming to mildly frustrate him, setting him up for a bad cop good cop routine, where I or Mrs. Jones would follow up with a soft spoken message of support, glamorizing a decision we ultimately wanted Cole to make for himself. Other times, I knew if Mr. Morales gestured towards the door, that whichever student we were supporting was likely to make a run for it. The bat that held my gaze as it lay against the wall was meaningful. It elicited a memory of the first crisis that earned my trust from Mr. Morales, a situation that would barely nudge my pulse now, as a weathered man of action. Though at the time, sneaking around building 18 unseen, and catching the bat thrown by an assailant as it rocketed towards Mr. Morales' skull was the kind of skill that was for hire. For some reason, there always seemed to be a poorly placed object laying around Bishop's campus. Either that, or these students had a particular knack for seeking such weapons out. And likewise, there were plenty of times Mr. Morales aided me in peeling a rabid child off my legs, or helped break up a fight that got overwhelming. But those are everyday occurrences, and hardly worth celebration. In my mind, what exalted Mr. Morales was so much more than this. Throughout these extraordinary situations, he always led by example. He remained composed, never lost his temper, and showed compassion towards children when most would have given up on them. I've seen him intervene in situations where he was egregiously assaulted by a kid who was uncontrollable, and yet a short time later, he would be found outside playing catch with the student, teaching him a lesson on how to perfect the curveball. He aided the teachers in every way possible, and his patience and understanding had far reaching effects not just for me, but for everyone that came in contact with him. He was the heartbeat of the school. His favorite saying was, "You can't write this stuff." The truth was stranger than fiction. The saying was the perfect reaction to all the chaos that would come to pass during my time at Bishop. I conditioned myself to accept and implement that mantra, for it always evoked an ironic laughter that allowed me to find some sort of wry amusement in whatever calamity had befallen me during my nine to five work day.

I returned the clipboard and closed the door to the closet after jotting down the pertinent information. Meanwhile Chad continued his tirade, "Ya'll are some stupid motherfuckers!" he would say as he wandered back and forth slamming the bathroom door. *He's still just a child*, I thought. It would do no good at this point to attempt to reason with him. Mr. Morales and I were implementing a strategy where we purposefully ignored him, providing minimal to no attention to the negative behavior on display so as not to feed in to it. Mr. Morales would cross the wood floor that needed mopping over to the opposite exit to ensure that Chad could not run out of the building. I would stay in proximity to the door we entered through, and here we would wait Chad out for however long it took. We knew the drill, this was the way of it, and we had executed this hundreds of times by now.

"Chris has __ in building 8 _____ removed," a muffled call over the radio. There were some staff that never learned how to operate their walkie talkies effectively. It seemed to me like a simple two to three step task. Make sure the line is clear, press the talk button down, make your statement, and do not let go of the talk button until you are done.

"Mr. Smith, you got to hold the button down the entire time you talk, we can't understand what you are saying," echoed the aggravated voice of Mr. Williams over the air. Mr. Williams was our office manager; upset because he is having to repeat himself again to Mr. Smith. He sat in the front office next to the antiquated intercom switchboard, which looked like something out of a 1980s Steven Spielberg movie with its series of oversized buttons, lights and switches. Mr. Williams was always lighthearted, quick witted, and good for a laugh. After being off all night, the office lights would warm up the room, bouncing off Mr. Williams' bald head as he greeted me with a fresh cup of java, "What's going on, Clark?" he would say. Sometimes he was weary from the night before. He held a second job as a taxi driver, which enhanced his playful character and supplemented his ability to counter jokes aimed at him, making his heckler wish he had kept his mouth shut. Mr. Williams seemed to enjoy his second job, he often boasted about how he made good tips. As several nearby colleges were known for their reputation as partying schools, he shared wild stories about how a group of good looking inebriated college girls would leave his cab in disarray. While I'm sure he enjoyed the tips, the job sometimes left him cranky in the mornings and "dog-tired" as he would say.

Much to my benefit and pleasure, Mr. Williams had even less tolerance for ineffective radio utilization than I did, particularly when he worked late the night before. He also had no qualms about expressing his disappointment over the air for all to hear. With a hint of annoyance, Mr. Williams would bitterly say, "Mr. Smith did you hear what I said? We can't make out what you're saying because you aren't holding the button down long enough. Get with the program."

Ironically, his own communication was somewhat muffled this day as he was talking with his mouth full, more than likely rounding out his routine pancake breakfast between fielding incoming phone calls to the office. No matter, it was clear enough, and it needed to be said. The importance of our communication system is invaluable. At any given minute there is a fire needing hosing down, you have to know how to request the hose, and Mr. Smith was always jamming up the airwaves with inconsequential concerns.

Mr. Morales and I would engage in informal dialogue with one another both to pass time and to let Chad know we weren't concerning ourselves with his behavior now that he wasn't a safety risk. Always looking the part, Mr. Morales would ruffle his black hair as he stood poised in his khaki pants and a green collared shirt that read "Bishop Secondary." He was approaching 40 years old but was still light on his feet. The students kept us in shape, and Mr. Morales, a self-professed baseball fan, often talked fondly of playing catch with his son or daughter to stay active.

"Catch the game last night?" he would say.

"You know I don't watch baseball," I said.

"Whatever you say gringo," he replied warmly. Mr. Morales was of Cuban descent and sometimes he would playfully insult me with Spanish slang. We would jest with each other out of the student's ear shot to retain our sanity.

Sometimes I wish I had logged my time in building 15 for the mere purpose of coming to some conclusion about what percentage of my life I spent in there. Curiously, it

65

was this building that I think of most when I reflect on my time at Bishop. It was this building that had an ineffective air conditioning unit that would slowly give way to the building becoming an intolerable sweatbox. I spent at least an hour a day in there with multiple students. It was not uncommon to have to manage a student in building 15 for five to six hours straight, depending on what mood they were in. Many of them were from low income, inner city neighborhoods with no reliable father figure around, and they spent their time outside of school running with the wrong crowds that led them to make poor decisions, in direct opposition to the teaching given at school. The power of their street culture was magnificent and we couldn't begin to hold a candle to the rush some of the less fortunate kids experienced from breaking the law with their peers on the street. Sometimes, no matter how hard we tried, we had to accept the fact that we had the students for only six hours a day, and then they spent the remaining eighteen hours unlearning everything we just worked on. Rinse and repeat. Hope that the message slowly sinks in.

Chad had developed a case of kleptomania. We would sometimes find wads of cash on him that he stole from unsuspecting adults who were fooled by his young, warm face. Other times he would unexpectedly consume Snickers bars and gummy worms he stole from the convenient store by his house. When you least expect it he would casually pull such items out of his pocket and enjoy his snack immensely, inviting questions from onlookers as to how he came by such a rare treat. This was especially frustrating at times when we were purposefully withholding reinforcement from him after a significant occurrence of aggression or a variation of property destruction. Bishop had a strict policy regarding any snacks that were awarded to a student for good behavior. First of all, we aimed for snacks to be healthy. Second, they had to be earned by means of appropriate behavior. As if to illustrate my point, Chad happened to pull a Snickers candy bar out of his pocket; needless to say he had not earned his consumables at this point. We knew this meant that he had most likely stolen it that very morning at a gas station. *Still just a child*, I thought. Chad started to unwrap the candy bar.

I really shouldn't allow this, I pondered.

He shouldn't be allowed to steal, curse out a staff member, slap me in the face, and then sit back and enjoy a candy bar. If anyone needs a candy bar, it would be me, I thought.

Given the nature of the job, one can quickly fatigue mentally from the perpetual agonizing complexity of navigating one's way to the best decision on behalf of the student. With so many emotional variables to consider, there is almost always a challenge at my feet, 1000 times a day it feels like. It was as if it was a never-ending game of mental gymnastics. Unfortunately, the best decision was usually the hardest, and one that the student was most likely to resist. I paused for a minute to compartmentalize my feelings.

I don't personally care that he stole the candy bar, aside from the fact that it is wrong. Check. The immediacy with which he consumes his candy bar post maladaptive behavior doesn't sit well with me. Check. Yet even then, I could simply ignore this behavior and store my energy for the inevitable round two with Chad which experience tells me is sure to come. Check. The thoughts continued to swim in my head.

"If anyone hears me, __ in build_ eight." Mr. Smith languorously attempted again to make indistinct calls for help, yet no one knew exactly what he was saying. Mr. Smith might as well have been on a forgotten mission to Mars, radioing earth for more resources and experiencing satellite interference. His unenthusiastic radio etiquette did little in the way of encouraging others to assist him. Mr. Morales would seize control, "Someone please walk to building 8 and find out what Mr. Smith needs," he said, condescendingly. Chad began kicking at the bathroom door with the bottom of his feet as he continued to unwrap his Snickers bar.

"I'm on it," an indistinct female voice over the radio. "Who's on it?" said Mr. Morales, "I couldn't make out who said that. Chad's banging on the door in here with his feet."

"This is Mrs. Jones," responded a comforting voice. "I'll take care of it."

Mr. Morales smiled, happy with the result, confident in Mrs. Jones' ability to deal with the crisis outside of building 15, which meant he could remain focused on Chad.

To avoid another mental disruption, I quieted my walkie talkie by turning my ear piece volume all the way down, which unexpectedly emphasized the sound of a fly buzzing around my head. My mind was racing at the sight of the candy bar, and I couldn't quite pinpoint the source of confusion.

Through the silence, and the intermittent sound of Chad kicking the door, I watched Chad fervently break in to the candy wrapper with his eager fingers. I felt unreasonably distracted by this, and frustrated at my attempt to understand why. (Bang, bang) Chad's feet kicked the door again. I stared at the candy bar, mystified, (bang bang), as the fly buzzed through the air (buzzzzz, buzzzzz). I clasped my shirt between my thumb and pointer finger and lifted it rapidly on and off my shoulders several times to cool myself off. *That candy bar is driving me crazy.* (Bang, bang) and the fly buzzed in the air, (buzzzzz, buzzzzz). The AC made a desperate attempt to kick on and cool the room, but rather than make the room colder the unit simply got noisier and added an obnoxious loud humming noise, (hmmm, hmmm). *I thought this was the chill room. Why does it have to be so damn hot?* (Bang, bang, buzzzzz, buzzzzz, hmmmm, hmmm,). *That candy bar is driving me crazy.* (Bang, bang, buzzzzz, buzzzzz, hmmm, hmmm,) and then nothing.

Not a sound for a brief moment. Time had frozen. *Aha.* Something clicked. I realized my source of mental befuddlement. It wasn't the candy bar that nagged at me, it was what the candy bar represented to me. The candy bar stared at me, laughing, Its corn syrup oozing down the side of the wrapper as Chad's face formed a smile that said he was quite satisfied with the way his day was going so far. Chad was representative of a sample of children who came from similar circumstances. I paused to think about how there had been a progressive confluence of national violence in school settings. There was a growing responsibility in the public's eye for educators, as well as mental and behavior health professionals, to curtail violent behavior. It seemed at this time as if every few months there was another catastrophic school shooting that made national headlines. The candy bar was the line that divided Chad and me. It was the division between generational gaps, technology advancements, cultural differences, and most importantly, the socially maladjusted child and the responsible adult. Not only was Chad diagnosed with emotional behavior disorder, he also suffered from depression, conduct disorder, and anxiety. This was it, I was on the front line of treating comorbid behavioral and mental diseases. It's not always as glamorous as it sounds. Did it all come down to this one decision over the candy bar? Was this the path to successful early intervention, or just a fool's errand? *I won't stand for this, I'll correct it,* I thought. I concluded that the more skilled Chad became at thieving, the farther and farther he slipped from his rehabilitation, which meant my back-breaking struggles with him in building 15 were futile. *I'll fight the good fight,* I thought, e*ven if that damn AC is broken I'm gonna make a difference.*

"Chad you stole that candy bar, didn't you?" I said inquisitively.

His cocked his head to the side and casually replied, "Yep. Don't give a shit."

That much is evident.

"Chad you need to hand me the candy bar, you didn't earn that, and you're lucky you weren't caught and arrested."

"You ain't getting my candy bar, come try and take it." He snickered.

"Come on Chad, you know what you did was wrong, let's get back to class and learn, then you can earn a snack from my office later."

"I'll eat this candy bar and then steal one from your office later. How ya like that pussy?"

I was nonplussed. *So much for my negotiating tactics,* I thought suitably.

Chad stared at me amusingly, self-satisfied, as if he had just discovered gold and there was some idiotic man trying to talk him in to giving it up. I took three authoritative steps forward and upturned my hand. Chad and I exchanged glances, he knew what was coming just as well as I did. He was almost halfway through his candy bar and time was running out. Chad looked at me fiercely, and tightened a kung fu grip around his prized possession. I leapt into action as he tried to deftly outmaneuver me. He feinted left, I didn't buy it, I opened both arms out wide to encompass a five foot radius from which he could not escape; there was nowhere for him to run. I moved forward one assertive foot after another until Chad was backed into a corner against the tree mural on the wall, the black and brown painted branches extending just beyond the top of his head every which way, as if he had walked right out of the very painting his back was now pressed against. With the tree branches coming out of his head, he realized there would be no escape, "Alright, take it ya bitch!" he said, as he snapped his head to one side.

I thought I would have to pry it from his fingers, but his grip loosened, and much to my surprise I calmly removed it from his fingers. *That was easier than it normally would have been.* Something was suspicious, as Chad routinely would have put up a much bigger fight. It was bait. I shouldn't have fallen for it, I should have known better. In exchange for the candy bar, Chad had cajoled me in to close quarters, plenty close enough to pull an old trick out of his sleeve. Chad made a hawking noise in his throat; I knew what was coming. I braced myself as my left hand took control of the candy bar, and brought my right hand up to cover my face, but no! Wait! My fingers had gotten wrapped around the wire to my walkie talkie, my right hand was now tangled in the wire similar to a fly caught in a spider's web, and I couldn't get my right hand free. I dropped the candy bar out of my left hand trying to make up the distance to my face, but it was too late, Chad spit a large wad of phlegm directly in my eye and began laughing hysterically. I was enraged.

The inevitable round two that I had accurately predicted just seconds before had officially begun. *Don't demonstrate frustration*, I thought. My blood boiled as I tried to stay resolute. Mr. Morales sensed my momentary disposition and moved in to take physical control of Chad, who suddenly realized his candy bar was gone forever, and began screaming and crying at the loss. Chad sank his teeth into Mr. Morales's right arm as if he needed blood to survive, and demanded, "Let me go Bitch!"

By this time I regained my composure, yet spit was still in my eyes and I was flying blind. With my blurred vision, we both escorted Chad to the safety room, a smaller padded area within the portable building, which measured approximately three to four feet wide and six to eight feet long. The room was used sparingly to place students in when they were too aggressive to manage even inside the chill room. Mr. Morales and I collectively peeled Chad's head back before his teeth could rip the skin of Mr. Morales' arm and draw blood.

There Chad continued to scream heinous yells. He squealed, squawked, hollered, and shrieked. All the while his nose ran snot down his lips, and tears streamed across his face, the only intelligible vocalizations made were "NO!" "NO!" "NO!" Mr. Morales and I had walked away and allowed Chad room to self-soothe. Better yet, I allowed myself the necessary room away from Chad so that I too could self-soothe, and clean my face in the bathroom sink while Mr. Morales kept a close eye on Chad. I hung my face down in the sink and splashed water on my face. *He's just a child,* I thought. The only other times I had heard screams like the ones Chad was making were on television, when a character such as a loyal wife learns of her husband's passing and suddenly falls to the floor, inconsolable and feeling agonizing pain. The level of emotion Chad displayed also made me think of the movie Cast Away, when Tom Hank's character is stranded on the desert island and befriends a volleyball, only to have his heart broken once again when the two separate at sea. Chad had parted with his candy bar, yet he wasn't acting, he was truly despondent.

Over the next fifteen to twenty minutes, Chad's cries gradually descended to a melancholy, downhearted whimper. All the while I would circle the room, wondering if I made the right decision. I hated to see Chad torn up like that, I just hated it. *Can't take it back now,* I said to myself, *the decision has been made, so stick with it.* But still, *why does this feel so wrong?* Finally Chad was quiet. I approached the small room where he was. He was a poor sight to see. Still shoeless, he sat with his back against the wall, smeared chocolate on his face, legs and arms outstretched as if he had just run a marathon. Perhaps his oversized t-shirt came in handy as a tool to wipe away tears that had gathered just beneath his lips and formed a small pond on his chin. *Still just a child.*

This was where the problem solving phase began. Sensing I could take things from here, Mr. Morales took his leave, hopefully to give Mr. Smith another crash course on how to use his walkie talkie.

Chad suffered from a lower than average IQ. In truth, I felt his intelligence subjected him to one of the saddest juxtapositions imaginable. He was intellectually delayed enough that it affected his problem solving, communication, comprehension, and his ability to form meaningful relationships, yet intellectually capable enough to be self-aware of these weaknesses. Chad could consciously acknowledge that he wasn't smart in the traditional sense of the word. It was like knowing that something is wrong with you, but never being able to figure it out, and so you are left wondering, always chasing something, but what? As a result, he internalized a lot of his low self-esteem and frustrated attempts to answer questions he couldn't quite grasp. He could hold a basic conversation, but as a seven year old who flourished on the streets of his neighborhood, school was scary for him. Reading, writing, sitting still, answering questions, all seemed like such a foreign idea. Even when he provided answers to questions, I could never be entirely sure he fully comprehended what was going on around him, much less the consequences of his actions. I thought of all the times I had watched him try to calculate two plus two on a piece of paper, subsequently putting his head down in yet another failed attempt. With all this in mind, I decided I had to be delicate with him, but firm.

"Chad, I'm sorry you are upset. What made you so angry this morning when you got off the bus?"

"Nothing," he would say heatedly.

"Chad, we can still turn this day around and have fun in class. Surely you don't want to spend all day on the floor?"

"No, nothing," he would say. I gave Chad a confused look. He continued, "nothing, nothing, nothing, nothing, nothing, nothing." He still retained the look of someone who had recently suffered a profound loss.

"What do you mean nothing?" I asked, slightly frustrated.

"Nothing!" he would shout.

"Chad when you yell, it makes me feel like you aren't ready to talk," I would say, soothingly. "I'll give you a minute to think about how you are supposed to talk to others, and I will come back to check on you."

"I got nothing now!" he said again.

"Nothing what?" I would persist, until I was almost yelling back at him.

"Nothing!"

"Chad help me understand so I can help you."

Chad repeated himself, "I got nothing I said!"

I pleaded with Chad now, "Okay...Nothing what?"

"For breakfast."

I paused.

"I got nothing to eat for breakfast," said Chad. "Mom says I don't deserve to eat. She says you're a rash, ain't worth my cash, and most of all you're a stupid piece of trash."

"You mean..."

80

"She don't feed me!"

And then it all became clear; my heart sank. This was the game changer. It was like being hit with a sledgehammer. If there was any residual anger towards Chad for the spit in the eye and the slap in the face, it was completely washed away. I was abruptly reminded that this was an entirely different playing field. Chad had been sent to school without any breakfast, as had happened so many times before. Stealing candy wasn't just a habit for him, it was survival. This was the whirlwind of behavior health, treating a child with so many complexities. He hoarded food because he never knew for certain whether he would be fed when he was home, and I had potentially just taken away his only meal for the last 24 hours. I began to concern myself with whether he had dinner the night before, there was no way to be sure. It was very likely the small bites of candy were all he had eaten. It would be worth a phone call to his mother; she would lie like so many times before and then threaten to sue us when the Department of Children and Families showed up at her house.

Chad looked up at me with wanting eyes. It was always difficult to discern whether he could be held accountable for his impulsivity. Several facts from his file stood out in my mind, "mother tested positive for crack cocaine at the time of birth, born premature, suffered collapsed lung, chronic asthma, possible fetal alcohol syndrome." It was always important to commit the files to memory, so we knew exactly what we were dealing with when trying to rehabilitate the students.

"Mr. Clark, I'm sorry," he would say. "I'm just trash," he muttered. I forced a difficult smile.

Was he sorry for the candy bar? The slap in the face? Or the spit in my eye? In terms of accepting accountability for any of that, the apology was all I could hope to get out of him. I tried to provide comfort by patting his back. Half an hour ago this room was filled with war cries from a battle that shook the earth. Now, the room was filled with sorrow, and the silence was deafening.

Breaking the silence, I said compassionately, "It will be okay. You're not trash. You are far from it. You are a good kid with a good heart. We just need to work on that pesky temper of yours." I meant what I said. Chad was a cute kid, and when he wasn't off his rocker, he had a likeable sense of humor. In the past he had talked excitedly about how much he wanted to fly a kite. Not too long ago, Chad had a period of three days in a row where he didn't have to spend any time in building 15. To make sure he knew I was proud of him, I bought a kite from a nearby store. It had an Egyptian blue color on half its width, complemented by a dark spring green on the other. When I presented the kite to Chad his eyes lit up like a million dollars. Elated, he was swept into youthful jubilation, with the kite in his hand he couldn't break his smile even if he tried. That day I watched him try to fly the kite in the fickle wind, imagining the kite was surfing the clouds, running through the tall grass in the fields between buildings, the thin white string awkwardly wrapped around his wrist and interlaced between his uncoordinated fingers, stumbling around from one step to the next trying to keep his untied shoes on his feet, frolicking, laughing, and free.

"Mr. Clark, I'm doing it!" he rejoiced. "I'm flying a kite!" In those moments, he was innocent and free spirited, euphoric and playful, like a child should be. He is not trash.

I'll make sure you eat buddy," and I moved to pat his back in an effort to comfort him again.

"Ouch!" he screamed as I patted his back.

"What is the matter?" I said, surprised by his reaction.

"That hurts!" he replied.

"Let me look at your back."

I stared at Chad's back with morose concentration. I was thinking how it wasn't uncommon for him to casually mention "the switch." Chad would sometimes reveal stories about the mischief he got into at his house. Punishment was his mother's answer to everything. If one is an attentive listener, one could establish a pattern with Chad's stories that almost always ended with, "Then I got the switch." In reality, Chad's mom was abusing him with whip like branches she broke off from trees in her backyard. Chad's own mother was intellectually delayed, her parenting skills were found wanting, and her on again off again boyfriend, known by Chad as "head buster," was in and out of jail.

As I lifted Chad's shirt, I could see his mother had been busy. The last time we confronted her about this, she blamed it on the neighborhood dogs. However, the long, horizontal scratches that stretched across the width of Chad's back, flashing hot red and pink tones under the light, never resembled claw or teeth marks left by a canine. Chad was seven years old and still not toilet trained. Despite some of his disabilities, he was fully capable of being taught to use a toilet appropriately, yet his mother never bothered. When he had an accident in his pants, he would "get the switch." Chad learned to avoid punishment from his mother by hoarding his feces covered underwear under his bed. Apparently, his mom had recently discovered the missing collection of underwear. I didn't need to ask; when you work with a victimized child long enough, you develop an instinct for this sort of thing. It was moments like these that put my life in perspective. *Some kids complain about not getting enough TV time.*

Chad's eyes were still red from sobbing and he looked physically ill. I reflected on the intensity of his crying just minutes before and I couldn't help but slip into an existential crisis for him. *Was it the loss of the candy bar that made him cry so? Was it pain in his back? Was it life? Had he suffered so much during his short span of life on this earth that he wept for all the years of punishment he had endured, for all the nights he was hungry or cold? Maybe he cried for all the times he outstretched his arms for a hug but found nothing but air? Perhaps it was for all the times he came to school with no laces in his shoes?* The rabbit hole runs deep.

This was a rare moment that comes full circle. Chad's life was constantly spinning out of control, it was a free-fall. This was normal for him. He didn't get to choose his preferences, he was never awarded nice clothes, never given the attention a child deserves. His mother subjugated him to whatever necessary, pernicious evils she felt he was deserving of. Chad was an excuse for food stamps, his world was as small as the block of public sector housing where he lived. School was the safest place in the world for Chad. More than likely, he would never know anything existed outside of what was directly in front of him in that very moment. Stealing seemed to serve the purpose of control. Alas, the candy bar wasn't just about satisfying a basic need for Chad, it represented the one thing in his life he had control over. Even if it was just for one speck of time, it was his to cherish. I deprived him of his moment where his world was still, his survival not threatened, a moment where he embraced the fact that, after all, he was still just a child.

I turned my radio volume back up just in time to hear Mr. William's announcement, "Attention all staff, we have a loose fox on campus, we are calling animal control. Do not approach the fox, I repeat, do not approach the fox, it could have rabies."

This is Bishop, I thought.

Chapter 3

Won it

The middle school students came pouring out of their classrooms, stampeding down the ramp of the portable buildings and aiming straight for me, while playfully wrestling over the football. All of them were eager to experience their five minutes of fame, daydreaming about that one catch that would elevate their status on campus to supreme athlete.

All students at Bishop struggled with their inability to demonstrate self-control. But the younger students were exponentially jaded in this category because of their youth and their naivety, and almost all had a comorbid diagnosis of attention deficit hyperactivity disorder and required constant redirection. Not everything in my job was stressful; part of my duties as a behavior analyst at Bishop was to have fun with the students.

After my stressful battle of the wits with Chad, it wouldn't hurt to throw around the pigskin.

For middle and high school students, the last five to ten minutes of each class was set aside for every student to participate in social practice time, more colloquially known as free play. This was, of course, barring any occurrences of broken noses or damaged property during regular class time. Free play was something that had to be earned. I thought about my childhood and how growing up I would walk a few miles to Winthrop Park with a group of my best friends, playing tackle football until the sun went down and we had our mothers worried sick. I remembered how free I felt, how innocent, careless and energetic. It was an escape, as if nothing in the world could ever go wrong. For these students, this was no different. They were hardly afforded an opportunity to do this outside of school. Who would they play with? A middle school student named Cole, for example, decorated his bedroom with bullet holes from his .22 caliber rifle when he got bored. Not your typical Saturday afternoon activity. They couldn't maintain stable relationships with kids their age. For some, the only friendships they had were the ones they tentatively formed at school, and due to the students' knack for violence, alliances were usually temporary and fragile.

This didn't always bode well for drama-free football games; if anything, it raised the stakes in a number of different ways. First of all, games were played on a thirty yard stretch of uneven ground between the portable buildings, with scattered patches of grass but mostly just dirt and the occasional pocket of rocks. If a student scored in the makeshift end zone, he immediately had to stop moving or his kinetic force would carry him straight forward and he would face plant into a 15 foot high metal fence. Though sometimes after scoring, the adrenaline rush came with superhuman abilities and they voluntarily rammed themselves into the fence for dramatic effect. Perhaps they fantasized about the fence being a field goal stand on an NFL field.

Second, there were only five to ten minutes maximum to create an effective football game with at least a few die hard touchdowns, before having to transition to the following class. This contributed to a tremendous sense of urgency to get the game going. Aside from the obvious problems with time constraints, the students spent half their free time bickering and arguing amongst themselves while trying to form teams and decide who was going to play quarterback. No sooner was a game formed than it was time for it to be over. Most students were never exposed to recreational sports of any kind, they were never taught a dose of teamwork or sportsmanship. It was hard enough for them to form a team without a brawl ensuing. Therefore, reminding them that they had poor time management skills sent them into a further panic and they would begin to behave franticly. Their entire body language would change, hands would be thrown up in the air, voices would elevate in pitch, and then the profanity would begin.

The last and most important aspect that raised the stakes was the grudges that were held after a game was finished. The students always had an ongoing territorial dispute over who was the reigning team. One has to remember that this particular population of students has a terribly low frustration tolerance. Contrary to what one might think, this made the football games important for invaluable teachable moments where I could redirect a source of hostility and turn it in to a friendly handshake. On the really positive days, the students would learn to congratulate each other for their effort and skill. Yet hundreds of opportunities across months of play would have to present themselves before the students were conditioned to this behavior. In behavior analytic theory there stood the concept of "learning history," it summed up an individual's history exhibiting a particular behavior. Usually the longer an individual's learning history with a specific behavior such as aggression, non-compliance, or overreacting to a peer who bumps into you during a friendly football game, the more time and effort it would take to correct the behavior. For now, when games were won by a group of students, this would likely lead to confrontations that would potentially spill over into the classrooms for days to come.

Zack was one student whom I had grown fond of. His family maintained a quiet life, away from civilization, and his dad held one of those hard labor jobs, though I was never sure exactly what. Zack was rotund, with wheat-colored hair, and a pale complexion to go along with his blue eyes. He had chubby cheeks smothered in freckles, and regardless of what the temperature was, he always rocked a black sleeveless nascar t-shirt, long blue jeans, and hiking boots. He was also known for his sarcastic sense of humor and witty remarks, albeit usually inappropriate, forcing me to laugh internally while simultaneously voicing my disapproval.

As serious as the kids took these games, Zack took it to a whole new level. Zack ran his heart out on that uneven hill every day. In his mind, there were collegiate scouts in the imaginary stadium filled with 80,000 people. Between runs Zack would pause to dump wood shavings out of his hiking boots, something he would pick up from working in the shop with his dad, his hero.

"Zack, how ya doing today?"

"Better now that I'm out of class," he would say.

"Did you work with your dad over the weekend?"

"Yep, he says he's gonna bump me up soon to use the saw all by myself." Zack's inflection in his voice lifted every time he talked about his dad, in spite the rumors that had been circulating about his father.

"Don't rush that," I said. Somehow I wasn't ready to trust Zack's temper with a saw in his hands.

As the students formed groups and huddled around to decide teams, I noticed Zack's normal sidekick, Cole, was missing. They both shared first period together with Mrs. Reese, the middle school math teacher.

Perhaps I missed something when I had turned my walkie talkie down in building 15, I thought.

"Zack, where's Cole?" I said. I always had to listen intently when Zack talked because he hadn't shaken the speech impediment that prevented him from pronouncing his Rs.

"He's sitting out this time, he fowgot his homewok for the thiwd day in a whoa, so Mrs. Weese had to give him a zewo. Then he got in Mrs. Weese's face and called hur a fucking slut," Zack mentioned ever so casually.

It was as if I simply had asked him how his day was going. The students had been conditioned to each others' outbursts at this point. Watching each other explode and curse out a staff member was as normal as the layperson getting caught in traffic. Teachable moment, "Okay so

Zack, next time I ask you what happened to Cole, and it's something similar to what you just described, you don't actually repeat the bad words back to me."

Zack's face looked as if he was disgusted with me. Now bitter, he would reply with a tone that insinuated *I* was the one who made the mistake, "Well you asked me what happened!"

"I did ask you, but you need to find a different way to say what you said. A simple, Cole got in trouble with Mrs. Reese would have been just fine," I suggested.

"Okay whatever let's get the game started," Zack said.

I wasn't totally satisfied with his response but I acknowledged he was trying to save face in front of his peers who were growing more and more impatient by the second. To stall the game in order to solidify my point with Zack would risk the threat of fifteen anxious students on standby becoming utterly fitful due to the ball not having been snapped.

The next 30 seconds unraveled quickly. I remembered some of the television videos I had seen at a social gathering one time where ESPN staff placed microphones in the professional football players' helmets during a game in order to capture all the smack talk exchanged by opposing teams. This really was no different.

"Cole's not here to save you today! Bet you drop that ball like I dropped my pants on your momma last night!"

"Keep talking shit and I'll bust your mouth open!"

"Alright watch me run laps around your slow ass!"

"Your mommas so fat that she hasn't left bed since she gave birth!"

"Well your mommas so fat she didn't even know she gave birth!"

"I will seriously kick your ass!"

"God why does your team suck so bad?"

"Man ya'll better stop fucking cheatin!"

"You guys can't catch shit"

"You ain't shit, Brian makes up your whole team!"

"All you do is give the ball to Devonte and let him run while you stand there with your mouth open!"

"You are so weak it makes me sick."

"This is my school, I am the shit and you are just a pile of dog crap."

As much as the students disliked one another in these moments, they experienced a dichotomy of emotions because throughout their contempt they were constantly vying for each other's approval. Competition was a syringe that penetrated their conflicted emotions, a catalyst to expose their twisted relationships. It was not a simple touch football game, it was life brewing up inside them. It was hard for me to keep up with all the calls. After 30 seconds, Sean, Jack, and Eddie were sitting out for teasing and using foul language; Craig and Mike were on warning for rough play; and Trevor had sprinted away from the area entirely and was now roaming the campus and kicking over trashcans, seemingly taking his revenge because the ball wasn't thrown to him right when he wanted it. Fortunately, he would be intercepted by a business-looking woman in a black dress and matching high heels. Mrs. Jones, who appeared to be carrying a vase full of fresh red and yellow flowers, seemed slightly downtrodden without her fixed smile that the students had grown used to. A mother of two, she had most likely used her nurturing, motherly voice to successfully convince Trevor to follow her inside to her office, where she undoubtedly would lecture him with both love and discipline.

Every game usually started out the same. It was important for me to weed out that day's rebels quickly and set the tone for the students that actually just wanted to have a few minutes of fun. I half expected things to get a little easier from this point. And then it came. Matthew hit Zack's weak spot, his kryptonite. He had taken a shot at Zack's dad.

"Zack, you can't catch a ball and your dad's an alcoholic!"

I felt the world shift. Zack's eyes glazed over; if it was possible, smoke would have come out of his ears. I had good rapport with Zack, despite the fact he had already been arrested for assaulting me with a chair months prior during one of his behavior meltdowns. If and when I could get him to calm down, he would own up to his mistakes and see reason. I immediately ordered Matthew to sit out for bullying, and requested that Zack join me at my side. I walked him to the side of a building where tears welled up in his eyes. Zack stood there, with his nascar shirt hugging his hips. I studied him for a moment, wondering who would talk first. After a tense moment passed, I asked, "Are you alright?"

"HE CAN'T FUCKING SAY THAT SHIT TO ME!" his chest rising and falling rapidly.

"I understand you're angry but don't curse at me please, I'm a staff member, that's your warning. Besides, just ignore him, he's only trying to get a rise out of you."

Zack tucked his head inside his sleeveless t-shirt and screamed, "THIS ISN'T FAIR!" as he fought back tears.

"Zack, take some deep breaths, you're heated right now because you've been running around. Take some breaths, try to relax, and don't say or do anything that is going to have you sent home," I said, calm and collectedly.

"I'M GONNA BEAT HIS ASS!" "HE CALLED MY DAD AN ALCOHOLIC!"

I would instantly regret the next words that came out of my mouth.

"Well, is he?" I asked somewhat sarcastically. I expected a resounding no to be the answer, which would then further our conversation and allow me to part the clouds for Zack by helping him find strength to ignore Matthew for saying something that was completely irrational and untrue. It was like so many moments experienced by me and other adults when you become stern with a child, banking all your money on their honesty and candidness to work in your favor so you can prove a point. Except Zack *was* honest. And he was the one that would prove a point. Instead of a confident "no," when I asked if his father was an alcoholic, I got a resounding, "YES!" he would scream.

Talk about your all time backfire. I thought. *Now I felt like a real jerk.* I wasn't entirely sure where to go from there, I had accidentally shut off communication. I watched Zack's sullen body language, it was as if he was being tortured by his inner demons, and even his demons had demons. He repeatedly pulled his head out of his shirt just quick enough to check and see if any of the other students were mocking him. Fortunately, they were preoccupied with continuing their disjointed football game. Zack moaned and rocked back and forth. He looked as if there was a full moon on the rise, and he foamed at the mouth as if he was cursed with lycanthropy. Any minute now he would inescapably morph into a werewolf, but in the meantime he was fighting it with every fiber of his being. Then I suddenly realized, he was genuinely trying to restrain himself from losing control. I had to tip my hat, I knew this was a tremendous accomplishment for him. Now it was time to do my job and salvage what I could.

"Sometimes when you are frustrated, the most constructive way to deal with it is to break a sweat," I said. Apart from the cursing and raging, Zack was actually handling the situation rather well, given his history. He had managed to keep his hands to himself, and as far as I could see, all school property within his proximity was still intact. This was actually a huge step forward for him. His chest began to fall lighter and easier, a sign he was calming down.

"Listen, you've had a good week, you are racking up all sorts of points for your good behavior lately, don't let this ruin your momentum. Let's move on together, what do you say? Let's go back out and win the game. I can even throw in some extra time later to pull you out of class early for us to pass the ball around," my attempt at trying to reinforce his somewhat appropriate de-escalation skills.

Normally I would have been calling for help on the air as I tried to peel Zack and Matthew apart, as one of them was sure to end up in a schoolyard headlock. For some of us, this type of violence ends as we mature into young adults and we reflect upon such moments at our ten year high school reunion and awkwardly laugh together. For others, it manifests itself as an avenue for all problem solving-strategies to converge. The violence carries into adulthood, when the individual is bigger, stronger, and more dangerous.

Just then I saw a twinkle in Zack's eye, a look I was unfamiliar with. It was somewhat mischievous and playful. He had stopped hyperventilating. He tilted his head to the side as if he had had an epiphany, a message from the gods even. It was a look of utter confidence. He had conceived a master plan, and was suddenly inspired. But inspired to do what?

"None of that will be necessawy, Mr. Clark."

"Okay, well what would you like to do?" I asked benevolently.

Seconds passed that felt like hours. The suspense was killing me. Zack remained steadfast. He looked up at me with fierce eyes,

"Won it..." he said.

Every word with an R in it reminded me of Zack's speech impediment. What he meant to say was, "run it."

Though I have no flair for the dramatic, I seized the height of the moment, and not wanting to let Zack down, I bought in. If this is what it would take to put this kid back on his feet today, I was willing to play along. I contributed to the theatrics of the moment, somewhat cautiously, playing in to the mystique.

I said, "Are you sure you want me to do that? It's risky."

"Won it..." he said again, with a look of determination. "Just won the damn ball..."

Nothing else needed to be said, I knew what play I would execute. If ever there was a time for impromptu theme music and a slow motion shot of a young kid in a sleeveless nascar shirt and an overly confident adult taking a walk onto a sorry excuse for a football field to wreak havoc, this was it. Zack had the eye of the tiger, and I wasn't going to let him down.

"What's the score here?" I said, as we re-approached the huddle.

"Were all tied up, time is almost out," responded Devonte.

I moved into the huddle with Zack's team. The students were bantering about trick plays, arguing over who would do what. None of their grand schemes ever produced the desired outcomes.

"Alright zip it and listen up!" I shouted. "Here's the deal. The ball will be snapped, I will be in shotgun position, I need two receivers on the right, and one going out for a screen pass on the left. Whoever gets open first gets the ball." What I didn't tell them was that actually none of them would get the ball. If I had been completely honest about my plan, they would've spoiled it before it could be hatched. Someone would have pouted about not getting the ball thrown to him, and deliberately sabotaged the play. I would captain the ship for the next 20 seconds, overriding whatever positions had been arranged without my consent. I stepped into the position of quarterback, took one last deep breath to scan the terrain as Zack lined up on my left. Mrs. Reese sounded the alarm for the transition to the next class, which meant we had time for just one more play. I tapped my right foot, signaling a runner to go in motion to throw off the defense. None of the kids responded to my non-verbal command because they didn't understand what it meant; I did, however, manage to step on a pinecone. I marked Devonte, who stared at me intently from across the line of scrimmage, which was actually just an ant hill. He was fast, and I would need to stay away from him.

"Down.....set....hike!" I shouted.

With the ball in hand, I executed a pump fake as if I was throwing to my right, the defense took the bait and shifted to their left. Then I sprang the trap; I was a horse exploding from his stable at the Kentucky Derby, and I immediately transitioned into a full sprint out of the gate. With a full head of steam, I dipped and dodged every flailing arm that came at me.

"Quarterback sneak!" I heard someone yell.

And the entire defense refocused their effort to hunt me down. It was like a pack of coyotes wanting to take down a moose. Owen, a scrawny sixth grader still growing into his shoes tripped over his own feet and fell down in front of me, *"Was he purposefully trying to sabotage our plan?"* I thought. *"No, he's just not coordinated."*

"Stay down!" I shouted at Owen, and I leapt into the air like a gazelle to clear his whole body as if it was a land mine that shouldn't be touched. I couldn't afford to be slowed down, Zack was counting on me. I was forming my very own highlight reel. By now I had cleared most of the defensive traffic, but there were two defenders left. I spun around in a 360 degree angle to beat the second to last and almost lost my footing. *These damn dress shoes were not made for this.* I recovered just in time to see that Devonte now stood between me and the end zone. To his surprise I ran straight for him, sacrificing myself. At the last minute, I turned my back to him and just before he tagged me with both hands, which would have killed the play, I flicked the ball to Zack who found himself in the perfect place at the perfect time. Zack gleefully caught the ball and ran unchallenged the rest of the way to the end zone. Never in history has a play come together so sweetly than when Zack and I pulled off the biggest sports upset of the century. Zack celebrated a victory dance and pummeled himself against the silver fence. He was grinning from ear to ear. I was happy to have contributed to his five minutes of fame.

Just afterwards, Matt approached Zack, and I braced for something unsettling to happen that would ruin Zack's moment. Much to my relief and shock, Matt held out his hand in textbook fashion, "I'm sorry for what I said man, I was just joking." he said.

Zack, riding his high, took his hand. "It's cool."

"Progress," I thought to myself.

"Never count these kids out, they are full of surprises."

Chapter 4

Woebegone

The sounds of Vehkavaara & Piltch's Mediterranean Nights tickled my ear drums. We were whipping around the winding terrain in my new, red Dodge Avenger. With the delightful guitar rhythms on the backdrop, I could have convinced myself we were in Spain had it not been for the endless cornfields that now surrounded me. The car wasn't exactly a sight for sore eyes, but it was my first V6 engine, and gave me enough confidence to edge out the speed limit without hesitation.

"How much farther babe?" I asked. "I'm getting hungry."

Fresh into our marriage, Brynn and I were exploring Willow Ridge Vineyards and Winery for a weekend getaway. Brynn smiled her infectious smile that made the freckles on her cheeks stand out just underneath her black Ray Ban sunglasses. She gave me a movie star look by taking her hand and dropping her glasses slightly down to make eye contact with me. "Just outside of Effingham," she said. "So not much longer." I knew that look, in spite of what came out of her mouth, it also meant "I love you, and stop asking me how much further." Then she turned her head to peacefully gaze out the window and her cheeks hid again just inside her long, alluring brown hair that smelled like a perfect combination of sensual vanilla and strawberry.

Within the next thirty minutes, we arrived at our destination. I narrowly escaped a collision with an RV that recklessly swung its way across the parking lot. The driver's face was obstructed, as the windshield was half covered by a paper map. Moments later, I couldn't help but reflect on my past. It had been roughly six months since I stepped off the Bishop campus. It was a necessary transition to further my career. With a local glass of red wine in my hand, I now stood on a beautiful patch of grass in Illinois, a far cry from the football field at Bishop where Zack and I made sports history. When the wind blew, my nose picked up the smell of something invigorating. The wind demanded that I turn my head and inhale. Fresh red flowers, not unlike the ones Mrs. Jones had carried in her hand from time to time, were flirting with my senses. I paused to appreciate the moment as Brynn tipped her glass against mine and said "cheers." As far as the eye could see, there were tantalizing patterns of multicolored flowers, and green vines littered with leaves that wrapped around stakes erected in the ground to promote proper growth of vegetation. I stepped forward, wanting to ingratiate myself with the endless rows of mesmerizing foliage that surrounded me. The moment, however wonderful, wouldn't last long. A child's roar pierced the air.

An odd place for a child, I thought. Several passerby showed displeased faces and rolled their eyes as if they had heard my thought and shared my sentiment. I glanced over my left shoulder as if to nonchalantly sneak a peek at the source of the distraction. With my experience in treating problem behaviors, I had become chronically obligated to analyze the behavior of both children and their parents. I told myself I wasn't judging, but I knew I was. I watched a family sitting at a round wood table decorated with wine glasses and cheese plate appetizers, underneath a pleasant canopy of trees that overarched a wooden deck. A child pushed the soles of his feet against the edge of the table, slouching back in his seat just enough to raise the two front legs on his black, grated metal chair, with a defiant aura about him. The mother and father wore brightly orange, sunny colored shirts with clashing blood red visors. Around their wrists weighed plastic bags that clinked and clattered indicating they had just left the gift shop. Everything about them screamed tourist. It didn't take much to note that it was their RV that inconveniently occupied half of the parking lot, no doubt. More than likely they were traveling across country and dragged their kid along for a good ole time.

"This wine is too fussy," pronounced the mother. "It just simply won't do." The father lathered his forehead in more sunscreen. In a joint effort, they both begged and pleaded with their child to eat the crackers they had packed for him. Not surprisingly, the child who was no more than four years old, had other plans in mind. He communicated this effectively through considerable protesting and hysteria. I began analyzing behaviors. The crackers, being a less preferred food, were saved until the end of his snack. The cheese that was presented on the table was eaten first by the child. This was a glaring mistake to me, as the child could have been motivated to finish off the crackers had the parents reversed the order of the food presentation. Their second mistake presented itself as the crackers were launched irritatingly from the child's hand onto the ground. Astonishingly, both parents would retrieve the crackers with utmost urgency, condemn one another, and place what was left of them into an impromptu trash pile within the child's reach, so he could repeat his behavior. The mother, flustered, tried to drink from her glass as she came out from under the table where she was picking up the cracker debris. Just before she rose from underneath the table, she clonked her head on the metal bar supporting the table that served little to no purpose for her son's lunch.

"OUCH!" she screamed in pain, trying to wipe the red wine from her mouth with one hand while grabbing her head in discomfort with the other. Publicly berating her husband, she quipped, "I told you not to pack these crackers, Ted!"

Embittered, the father said, "I wouldn't have packed them had you not rushed me out the door! Besides he always eats the crackers when it's just me and him, he's not eating them now just because you're here!" Cried her husband defensively, "So don't chastise me Debra!" The man dragged out his wife's name, as if he was dragging her through the dirt.

I tipped my wine glass back more earnestly now; things were getting good. The child reveled in his success, and my social graces were challenged. At the thought of being publicly vilified, the mother's eyes turned to fire, "What does me being here have anything to do with whether or not he eats the crackers, hm? Oh and maybe if you learned how to drive I wouldn't have rushed you out the door, Ted!" She returned the favor of stretching her husband's name out as if to punctuate his perceived stupidity in her eyes.

Peeved, both parents threw their hands in the air, then suddenly shot me a sharp look. *Perhaps I hadn't been as inconspicuous as I thought, or even worse, had I accidentally laughed out loud and not realized it?* What I thought appeared to be a look of disdain, turned out only to be a look of frustration and embarrassment. Both parents, remembering they were in public, had silently resolved to agree to disagree; a welcome decision for nearby wine drinkers.

Sheepishly, the father's eyes met mine, "I spank him all the time but it doesn't seem to work," He said.

If I had a nickel for every time I heard that, I thought.

***

Chad's mother stood in front of me.

She shifted her weight from one leg to the other, her black flip flops sparkled with jewelry on the straps between her toes and she stood with one hand on her hip propped to the side. Her black pajama pants were decorated with the fictional tweety bird cartoon character doing backflips up and down her legs. Her midsection was too large to be contained by her pink shirt, and her stomach fought with her waistline as if it was imploring her for more room and fair treatment. She had the look of someone who rarely left her plausibly insalubrious environment that she called home. Her hair was in disarray, though she brushed it as she gave me orders, fully believing it was fixable. Meanwhile, her large breasts sagged over her stomach and were poorly hidden by her shirt, leaving little to the imagination.

Predictably, Chad had made his way back to building 15 with Mr. Morales due to another rule violation. I had just washed my hands and contemplated finishing that cup of coffee I started earlier. It was just before 11:00 am. *I'll spend all day chasing this cup of coffee.*

"Bring him to me!" Chad's mother demanded.

"Yes ma'am. But before I do, something the matter?" I said.

Her eyebrows furrowed. "As a matter of fact, that damn boy stole money from me again! I'm gonna whoop his ass!" she said pointedly.

Here we go again. I feared for Chad. I was in an odd place, between a mother and her son. Whether she was right or wrong, he was her son and she would be the leading authority despite what others thought.

I looked at Chad's mom inquisitively, "How many times has this happened now?"

"Too many damn times! I spank his behind every time I catch him but it don't work! He turns around and steals from me every day!"

The relationship Chad's mother maintained with the school was tumultuous at best. Our administration had placed several phone calls to the department of Children and Families in cases where we suspected abuse. Although the calls were anonymous, Chad's mother quickly concluded their source, and the finger was always pointed back at us. Just as his mother constantly intimidated Chad with threats of violence, so did she threaten a lawsuit against the school for making what she felt were false accusations.

"I would advise against that ma'am. We need to figure out why he keeps stealing, teach him it's wrong, and why it's wrong." *It would help if you developed some organizational skills and stopped leaving money laying all around the house within arm's reach of him,* I thought.

"Go get my son, I'll be waiting here."

I turned to walk down to get Chad, not sure how the next few minutes were going to play out. His mom had come up here before. While she missed parent meetings, teacher conferences, and open house, she always showed up when Chad angered her enough, and there was always hell to pay for anyone involved. My mind was racing back and forth with all the possible outcomes, when a casual voice interrupted my thoughts, "Did you know that Axl Rose is an anagram for oral sex?"

"Oh my dear lord! I don't even know how to respond to that right now," I snapped, caught off guard. "That's wildly inappropriate and not something you talk about, Grant," I scolded him. He had snuck up behind me with his uncut hair and sandals, Ramones T-shirt and camouflage pants picking up pieces of grass as he clumsily walked my way, seeking the joy of discussing his musical database knowledge with me. I felt bad for having reacted with such disgust. Half the time Grant recites these facts to give him comfort in a conversation, but he doesn't understand the things he says, which makes it difficult to hold him responsible.

"What's oral sex?" he asked innocently.

"This conversation is over before it even began. Go to class."

I made a mental note to speak with Grant's parents about some of his facts he enjoyed discussing so much. But for now, there were more pressing matters. I returned to the sultry stench of building 15, popped open the door and turned the corner expecting to converse with Chad about the money he allegedly stole from his mother's purse. I was flabbergasted when the bathroom door flung open behind the force of Chad's foot, as if he had channeled someone much stronger and older than himself. Behind the door emerged Chad, wielding a tightly gripped shower rod in both hands. Chad had apparently requested to use the bathroom, and Mr. Morales gave him a chance to do so without creating any problems. Chad's creative appetite for destruction had taken over once again. Immediately, he began swinging the shower rod at our shins as if he was hacking down a tree.

Every day at Bishop I experience something new. I could now check off "victim of assault with a shower rod" from my bucket list. I instinctively jumped out of the way as the shower rod came within inches of my kneecaps. With the rod in hand, Chad extended his reach by about 6 feet. Fortunately, Chad wasn't yet coordinated enough to find his mark with much grace. Mr. Morales and I tap danced and dodged as if we had stepped on a hot bed of coals and someone was throwing firecrackers at our feet. Between swings, we both tried to catch our breath and command Chad to stop, though we weren't able to get a hand on him.

"Your mo__"

(gasp)

"Stop, your mother__)

(gasp)

"Chad, your mother is here!" I insisted.

Chad froze with a look of panic, as if he was a deer caught in headlights. The air inside building 15 was familiar of course, but the shift in energy was transparent. He dropped the shower rod, completely deflated. He had done a remarkable 180 degree turn and returned to wailing and sobbing as he had done just over an hour ago. I immediately knew that Chad knew why his mother was there, and was already visualizing the consequences of his actions.

How hard it must be for a child to both love and fear his own mother, I pondered. Although this was not your typical form of fear, such as fear of being reprimanded, fear of being grounded, or missing out on play time with friends. Chad's fear was the kind of fear he felt to the core of his being.

Her established pattern of domination using strategies that were completely irrational was about to continue. Time and again, she would place completely illogical demands on Chad, isolate him, emotionally abuse him, and neglect him. There was always the constant lingering threat of physical violence if Chad stepped out of line. Chad's idea of self-respect had been deteriorating since birth. He felt this unrequited love for his mother, a love matched only by his fear of her abuse, which actively thrived under the guise of discipline.

After I debriefed with Mr. Morales, he encouraged Chad to turn the money over. Chad insisted he didn't steal anything, although in his head, he must have already known the outcome of this situation. By this point in his life, he was programmed to lie. With his mother's presence on campus, he sensed the severity of the circumstances, and as he went through the motions of denial, he did so with far less passion and vigor than what is considered a normal performance for him. No Oscar awards for best actor would be given today.

"Check my pockets," he said, frightened, and still hoping to dodge the inevitable bullet. His shoulders slumped, eyes pointed to the floor, Chad turned out his pockets on both sides of his legs and his backside also. He was empty.

"Chad...take off your socks," said Mr. Morales.

Still protesting, he screamed, "NO! I didn't do anything!"

Mr. Morales pleaded, "Chad if you didn't steal anything you have nothing to worry about. If you did, you won't be in as much trouble if you tell me now. We can talk to your mom and tell her that you admitted to stealing."

Chad's anxiety was palpable; he began sweating from fear, as if he was suffocating from the very air around him. Stubborn and shaken, he appeared defeated and helpless. Somewhere within the depths of his brain, he trusted Mr. Morales's reasoning. I learned a lot of what I know from Mr. Morales; namely, how to be a kind, trustworthy individual, who was consistently patient, and ultimately, a very reinforcing and positive person to be around. On an instinctive level, Chad understood this as well.

The tension we felt on behalf of Chad filled the room. Time lingered on, and Chad's mother didn't like to be kept waiting. His facial expression slowly, painfully changed from a look of denial to a look of acceptance. Somewhat hesitantly, Chad reached down in his left dirt stained sock ever so carefully. A flash of green appeared, then disappeared, then reappeared again as his twig-like fingers fumbled in and around his ankle. Finally, Chad's hand came out of his sock, and in it was a folded, crumpled up fifty dollar bill. He stared at the ground, and extended his arm with his hand turned upwards, signaling to Mr. Morales to take it. Chad, having no concept of money, more than likely would've gotten a sour deal with his currency, trading it to one of the older students on campus for something as trivial as a piece of gum or broken headphones.

"You did the right thing just now, Chad," who stood with his shoes still untied.

Mr. Morales pocketed the fifty dollar bill for the walk up to Chad's mother, and turned his head to the exit contemplatively. "Give me just a couple minutes then walk him up to his mom," said Mr. Morales. He marched across the dirty floor, the wood creaking with each step, and left the building, brainstorming ways to diffuse Chad's mom for his sake. I looked at Chad and he appeared as if he was someone who had already been convicted of a crime, he now stood awaiting his sentencing in court.

Several minutes later, I walked him towards the front office where his mother waited, but I took my time, hoping that with each passing second Chad's mother would calm down. The entire situation foreshadowed Chad's fate. Oddly enough, this was hardly the first time this had happened. Despite our nudging her to keep her money in a safe spot, Chad's mother often lost track of it as she left it strewn throughout the house, which played out as the ultimate teaser for Chad to act on. Yes, her son has problems with stealing and impulsivity, but you don't starve a dog and then dangle a steak in front of his face expecting him not to eat.

As we approached Chad's mom, we found her standing where I left her, hulking over a tree with her hands on its limbs. She was snapping a thin branch off of one of the branches, a makeshift switch, portending how the next few minutes of Chad's life were to play out. She angrily glared at Chad, "Get over here trash!" she commanded.

Was she really about to try and do this on school campus in front of everyone? I thought.

Mr. Morales stood close by, though I was still too far away to make out what was being said. I held on to Chad's hand. It was moments like this where I was willing to overlook all the times Chad had punched, kicked, slapped me, thrown miscellaneous objects at me, and even spit on my face.

Still just a kid, I thought.

"Chad, get your ass over here!" his mother screamed. She stood brooding, flexed, and if I didn't know any better, I'd say she was foaming at the mouth. Chad's grip in my hand tightened, he was uncharacteristically quiet. I wanted to give him a hug and tell him it would be okay. I noticed he was now walking behind me, his pace had progressively slowed down, his shoulders slouched, making himself as small as possible, any smaller and he would've been invisible and faded into thin air. As we closed the distance between the four of us, Chad tried to bolt in fear, but still attached to me, I restrained him with my hand in his, as he began whimpering and protesting. "I don't wanna go..." "I don't wanna go... I'm sorry."

"Don't you even think about running from me!" his mother screamed irately.

I noticed my pace also slowed down to match Chad's, *even I* felt afraid of what was to come. Chad's mother now marched toward us, as Mr. Morales followed closely behind, trying to talk her down. My body felt stiff; I hated this moment. I didn't know what to do. *What are my boundaries? How do I come between a mother and child?* I thought. It felt wrong, as if I was returning a wounded, defenseless deer into the wild, where it would surely be eaten alive by wolves within the hour. Everything was so backwards. Reluctantly, I broke contact with Chad's hand, turning it loose, and handed him off to his mother. But the last second as I pulled away, my two longest fingers accidentally grazed the outside of Chad's hands one more time, and in that second I felt his fingers stiffen with rigor mortis like rigidity, a tell-tale sign of abuse. It was that second we grazed hands that told me more about Chad than all my hours in building 15 with him. Deep down, he was a scared, lonely boy who wanted sanctuary. Continuing our pattern of non-verbal communication, Mr. Morales and I exchanged a confused look as if to say, "Is this really happening?"

Once in her custody, his mother forcefully turned Chad's body away from her and raised her right arm that held a thin switch approximately three feet long and less than an inch in diameter. "The thinner ones can whip faster," she said. She wielded the weapon with a religious passion, as if it was a sword, and she was fully prepared to do God's work. As she extended the thin switch over her head in an upward motion, it made an evil whipping noise. Chad was streaming tears and braced in anticipation of the crackling pain he was expecting any second now.

A powerful male voice stood out, "Stop right there!" Mr. Morales shouted. "Have you lost your mind? You can't do that!"

Chad's mother looked insulted. If I could have placed a thought bubble above her head it would've read, "Who the hell do you think you're talking to?"

"I can discipline my children any way I want! If he don't learn now, how's he ever gonna learn? This boy needs a whooping!" she said.

"That's exactly the point. I've been telling you for years," Mr. Morales said. "Chad doesn't learn this way. He doesn't understand. We need to find other ways to teach him."

The bell signaling the students' transition to their next class rang loud and clear. It bought everyone a few more seconds to consider their options. A crowd mixed of students and staff had now begun to form in the parking lot to watch the commotion. Chad's mother, now acknowledging that she was under the watchful eye of school administration, reluctantly dropped the switch. She looked down at her feet, as if she was deliberating on an alternative approach. Much to everyone's bewilderment, she settled for what she felt was a lesser form of punishment, and had somehow managed to convince herself it was equally as acceptable as her previous plan.

She bent over, moaning in frustration, either at Mr. Morales' interruption, or at being forced to bend past her own waist. As she reached down to her feet, she peeled her black, jewelry laced sandal off her right foot, raising it now just as she had done with the makeshift switch seconds before. She gripped Chad's hair in her hand, effectively controlling his body, and slamming him against the same tree where she located the switch just seconds prior. Chad's head bounced off the wood pine with a disgusting thud, yet he had been conditioned not to protest or scream, he knew better than to make a sound. Several pieces of tree bark tumbled down the back of his shirt. He was her piece of trash.

"Don't gotta use a switch to get the job done," she said with a sinister tone.

Again, I heard a very powerful "NO" from Mr. Morales. "What are you doing? How can you think this is a good idea?" Chad's mom thought that going from a switch to her footwear would somehow placate the laws of abuse on a school campus.

"Our school deputy is just inside the office," shouted Mr. Morales, his Cuban blood running hot. "I'll have him out here immediately if you keep this up!"

I was still trying to process what was unfolding before me. I was in shock. Chad's mother had worked herself up into such a frenzy she was going to publicly beat and humiliate her child for all to see. This is the problem with perpetual punishment, it gives the punisher a sense of irrational justification, thereby making it as addictive as a drug.

Chad's mom scoffed at the threat of the deputy getting involved. But it was enough to quell her anger for the moment. She was outnumbered. She grabbed Chad by the shirt and manipulated him across the parking lot into the backseat of her rusty blue Buick, one shoe still off. *Runs in the family I guess.* Chad sat in the backseat, staring out the window with a numb expression. His placed his hand with all five fingers against the window of the backseat. His crestfallen brown eyes met mine as his lips pressed against the glass. I stood still, unsure of what to do or say, just watching his eyes. Suddenly he made a fist and began pounding on the window repeatedly, signaling he wanted to escape. He wanted saving. He mouthed something to me that made my knees weak, "Help me. I'm trash. Help me. I'm trash. Help me."

That woman is pure evil.

Chad's body was jarred away from the window and flung about the backseat as the Buick tires screeched and burned rubber against the asphalt. There was a rupture of applause from onlookers as Chad's mother sped away and nothing was left but a cloud of car exhaust. Mr. Morales turned to look at me, "You can't write this stuff..." he said. Only this time, the comedic irony had left his voice, and his tone was replaced with that of a sad, morose timbre. The masterpiece of a moment was brief. It was one small victory in an age-long battle. *Did we make things better or worse? Did we save him from a beating, or set him up for something far worse when he gets home?* Chad's safety wouldn't be guaranteed once he left the campus. The probable outcome of his evening was that he would go to sleep tired, hungry, and unloved. In the morning, daylight would climb the walls, and Chad's living nightmare would start all over.

Chapter 5

Zahra and her baby

For a few seconds I thought I had gone crazy when I heard the sound. My ears perked up and I was being drawn to the noise of what sounded like an infant. The sound drew me closer to portable building number 5. In typical fashion, a proper sign could not be afforded. Instead, a single piece of paper with the words "Life Skills" printed on it was taped to the door next to a black number 5 shadowed by white outline. I wondered, *Why is our school so forgotten? Why is that we print signs for our doors when other schools have them engraved with haughty looking font? Is it because if we spent money on a nice sign for our door, we wouldn't be able to keep the electricity on? Is there anyone up at the district level that cares about this place? Somewhere, there had to be someone with a suit and tie who had the power to infuse positive change in our school. If only they would look this way.* Amidst the baby's cry, I quietly reflected on how many times I'd overheard the principal discuss upgrades to our school, and how she wasn't getting any support from the superintendent's office. "They're working on it," she would always say, which was essentially the same thing she said last year, and the year before that.

I bumped in to Mr. Morales, who was attempting to perk himself up after the parking lot confrontation with Chad's mother. He quipped, "Want to bet Lindy's famous 12 piece chicken wings the day doesn't get crazier than this?"

"Something tells me it will, based on the way it started. So you're on."

I continued walking towards the noise to locate the source. I found relief in my ability to attest to what I heard seconds prior, and indeed I was not crazy. A window was cracked to the classroom, I could see perfectly inside as no furniture obstructed my view. A baby, no more than one year old, clung to the neck of his mother, our student, Zahra.

The classroom portables at Bishop left much to be desired. From outside, one could see decor you would typically expect from a life skills classroom. It was just adequately decorated with large posters of typical role models, such as Michael Jordan, Thomas Edison, Albert Einstein, and several more. On the shelves lay a messy array of several cookbooks for when the students learned how to prepare meals. One could note the mangled pages that stuck out, and barbeque sauce stains that splattered across the cover of the books. Just across from the shelves with cookbooks rested a large, stainless steel sink with a leaky faucet, a beat-up, rusted, white refrigerator with black handles, and an electric coil stove top with missing drip pans. The noisy AC unit attached to each portable was inactive long enough for me to hear the cries of the child, observing surreptitiously without interfering.

Zahra was not the first student at Bishop to have a child during high school, but she was one of the youngest, barely out of middle school during pregnancy. Zahra loved to perform nice deeds for others, such as making beads and necklaces for her friends and teachers, or passing playful notes during class, which sometimes got her in trouble. At heart, she was a sweet, caring, innocent child, still years short of her eighteenth birthday. In spite of this, her looks and outwardly, aggressive, hypersexualized behavior aged her image considerably. Zahra had a history of sexual abuse and was a frequent violator of the dress code. Rightfully so, I never personally addressed her dress code mishaps. Sadly, she would have enjoyed the attention. Her history of abuse led to lack of impulse and control, distorted perceptions of reality. She repeatedly placed herself in promiscuous situations with older males, which led to her victimization. Knowing this, I steered clear of her, deferring to female staff if Zahra required someone to talk to. In truth, it was uncomfortable for me to even make eye contact with her for fear of her misinterpreting the behavior of a respectful, male adult.

Notwithstanding childbirth, Zahra was truly street hardened, and not surprisingly, had a nefarious temper that landed her at Bishop. Though normally jovial and pleasant, one could compare her anger to throwing a hand grenade in the middle of a crowd. She would launch into a primal tirade, yelling, shouting, and cursing with her hands in the air; nearby people would scatter, and onlookers would watch in horror. As I watched her with

THE MISFITS

her child, I couldn't help but remember an occasion when Zahra attacked Devon, a male student, for calling her a "stupid ass" during a kickball game in P.E. class. This occurred prior to her child's birth, when she was seven to eight months pregnant. Like a deranged tyrant, she sprinted across the clay and leapt over third base to land a right hook on the side of Devon's face, calling him a "mother fucker." She threatened to have her gang banger cousins "put a hit on Devon," if he ever cursed at her again. What's more, her impressive ability to self-soothe just as quickly as she escalated often left onlookers befuddled. After all the examples I had seen of her with intense rage followed by immediate, quiet solace, my confusion with the drastic range in emotions was consistent with the opinion of others. In this instance with Devon, after exhausting her aggression, she briskly walked into the dugout and stretched out on the bench for some rest and relaxation, as if nothing remotely significant had passed. Devon, a good foot taller than Zahra, stood stunned, and appeared in fear for his life. Not knowing what to do, he buried his face in his hands, began bawling, and ran away in shame for having been

137

beaten up by a pregnant girl in sandals. As if the sneers and jeers from other students weren't enough, Zahra could be heard from the dugout saying, "Stop crying baby," as she laughed contentedly with herself. Sometime later, I had to track Devon down in the bushes of a nearby house. I thought of how the situation grew tense, the skies turning dark grey and black, as if someone had injected smoke across the heavens, prompting lightning bolts to propagate the clouds in angry, jagged streaks of scintillating rage. Against my better judgment, I recalled how I tried to cajole Devon back to campus by telling him that not many people really saw what happened, which wasn't actually true. I felt bad for lying as surely that detail would hit a snag, but assumed that technicality could be dealt with once back on campus. But despite being known for her rage, it was the caring side of Zahra that allowed her to retain a sort of youthful innocence. Such innocence had always prompted her to come back and pick up the pieces of her mess. I remembered trying to help solve Devon's problems while he lay in the bushes, red-faced and basking in shame. Devon had completely balked. *How will I talk him back on campus after what just happened?* I thought. Just then, Zahra unexpectedly approached us from behind. I instinctively thought Zahra would be the last person Devon wanted to see, as he retreated further into himself, tucking his legs back under the green branches that dropped leaves on his goofy face. But then, "I'm sorry, Devon," Zahra would mutter. If they were two puppies, she would have gently pawed at Devon to make sure he was okay, and Devon would have scratched his ear and stuck his nose out from under the bushes to see if it was safe. There was no sense that Zahra was baiting Devon into some sort of cruel joke. Her apology was heartfelt; she had lost her tone of mockery, and, feeling truly bad for embarrassing Devon, had come to make amends. Contrary to what I first thought, I realized that Zahra was the *only* person who could convince Devon to come back to the school grounds. Sure enough, Devon returned the apology, and the three of us made our way back just before the sky fell out. From that day forward, Zahra took Devon under her wing, and anytime someone brought up the incident on third base at the kickball field, Zahra threatened them with severe bodily injury. It was her own twisted way of living up to her apology, while rejuvenating Devon's reputation.

From what I understood, Zahra, at her young age, was deemed an unfit mother by her legal guardian, social worker, and the court system, but granted visiting time by her grandmother, who ultimately provided care for Zahra's child. Once or twice a week, Zahra would spend an hour or so with her child under the supervision of responsible adults at the school. At the moment, Zahra was practicing comforting her restless child to sleep. Mrs. Rehder, a grandmother herself and part time teaching aide, was explaining the process of calming the child down. Although well intended, Mrs. Rehder sometimes missed her mark with the unique student population at Bishop. She was a frail, elderly woman, who was soft spoken yet sometimes took too much time to make a point, wearing on the students' patience. Most students won't stick around for a lecture, and Mrs. Rehder got sidetracked so easily she would forget what she was talking about midway through her sentences. She employed a kind of "put a nickel in the swear jar mentality," which often left her out of her element, rendering her confused and overwhelmed by the fast paced, frequently hostile environment. Although ultimately she was a pushover, her redeeming quality was unending patience. Fortunately for Zahra, patience is exactly what was needed. As I looked on, Mrs. Rehder continued to talk through the steps needed to soothe the crying baby.

Zahra sat impatiently, with her cutoff jean shorts and black tank top that just barely met the minimum "three finger width" requirement on her shoulders. If ever one has looked such an unnatural mother, it was now. Zahra's body language indicated she was afraid of her child, as if she was holding a bomb, and touching him too much may set off an explosion. Frantic, she refused to make more than minimal physical contact with the baby, only offering a cold hand and a sideways glance. As she held the screaming boy's arm with her left hand, the young infant balanced his fate on the edge of his mother's lap. The baby twisted and contorted his body in the shape of an uneven backbend, wrapped agonizingly around his mother's arm, screaming as he desperately yearned to be comforted properly. "Shut up!" screamed Zahra. "Won't you just shut up?" she said aloud. Mrs. Rehder did her best to warm Zahra up to the idea of soothing the child as opposed to berating him. But Zahra didn't know any better, being told to "shut up" was what she heard her entire life from her own mother, who no longer had legal custody of her.

"Now, now dear, remember shut up isn't one of the S words we talked about. We can swish, swaddle, swing, shush, or give him something to suck on, but we don't say shut up. And let's use two hands while we're at it." Mrs. Rehder adjusted her yellow, lemon colored summer dress and let her arms collapse into her lap. Her pine needle colored hair rested on her delicate, frail shoulders. On the table next to her lay her straw hat that she wore when walking between buildings. In the hat rested a bottle of sunblock, labeled SPF 50. She lived in constant fear of being sunburned and had to keep her skin protected at all times.

"How about you take him, because I'm getting tired of this. Seems like all he do is cry," said Zahra.

"No dear, give it one more try, you can do it. Let's swing him back and forth gently." Mrs. Rehder lovingly placed Zahra's hands where they needed to be to calm the infant down. Zahra relaxed ever so slightly as Mrs. Rehder guided her appropriately. She let her left arm rest underneath the baby's bottom and support his weight, while her right arm cupped the back of his head. The bond between mother and child appeared unnatural. But what could one expect from a 15 year old mother, just getting used to the idea of being a teenager?

It was rumored that the father of the child was in his mid-twenties, and found his way into Zahra's house as a "friend of the family," who needed a place to lay low for a while until his gang feud passed over. When Zahra became pregnant, the father fled the state, never to be heard from again. He had been picked up by law enforcement for assault with a deadly weapon several states over, and was awaiting his court date. More than likely he was looking at jail time for his crimes, as he could offer no child support and the judge would not look kindly on his relationship with a minor.

"Shhh, shhh!," voiced Zahra, impatiently.

143

"That simply won't do," said Mrs. Rehder. "Softer dear, let him feel your love."

"Shhh, shhh," whispered Zahra, still impatient but slightly more forgiving.

"You're getting it," Mrs. Rehder voiced in approval, nudging her to continue.

The child's disruptive cry turned to a medium bodied protest, and Zahra almost looked satisfied. Something began to click.

"I don't have his pacifier," Zahra said.

Mrs. Rehder graciously searched through the child's bag of belongings, shuffling through diapers, empty formula bottles, and a change of clothes, but came up empty-handed.

"I don't see it in here. See if you can just improvise," she said.

"What do you mean improvise?" asked Zahra. "What does that word mean?"

"Just...do your best." Mrs. Rehder responded, as if a further explanation would confuse Zahra.

They say a picture is worth a thousand words. The next thing to happen was a subtle moment in time that would unravel itself as a bittersweet picture never to be forgotten. Perhaps it was Mrs. Rehder's patience and persistence, or maybe it was an instinctive moment that finally registered with an inexperienced, disinclined mother. But something inspired Zahra to grasp her child's thumb, and place it in his own mouth. Upon doing this, the motherly gesture was met with instant success. When the baby's crying dissipated, a look of relief swept over Zahra and a proud smile crept on her face. Her shoulders went from tense, to relaxed. Suddenly able to focus, she felt a new sense of purpose and took advantage of the rocking chair, she began gently rocking back and forth.

Mrs. Rehder echoed an excited whisper, "You did it dear!" as she nodded in approval.

However, what followed would be an image that demonstrates the irony of Zahra's quandary. It would pass as the ultimate representation that a mother is not ready for a child, a disturbing reminder of how small the intellectual maturity gap is between Zahra, and the living, breathing baby that now rested in her arms. As I silently celebrated for Zahra, she took her hand off her baby's head, and eagerly placed her own thumb in her mouth. The corollary came to pass, as mother and child sat quietly, each sucking on their own thumb. A disheartening affirmation that poor Zahra was not that far removed from childhood herself.

Chapter 6

The Ring of Fire

"They need Deputy Richards in building 16 pronto!" I followed the bread crumb trail of toppled trash cans which lead me to a cacophony of noise taking place in the high school class. Although I pitied the students for having a glorified trailer park for classrooms, the one fortunate characteristic of this building type, ensured that any time there was a tussle going on inside, the ruckus could be heard from fifty feet away. Any staff member who happened to be nearby didn't have to think twice about what was unfolding, and could put themselves in a position to assist. Outside the room, all students had cleared the building following the teacher's orders, the protocol for when one student goes berserk and refuses to leave the room, endangering others.

Inside, I watched Deputy Richards and Kenny square off. *Here we go.* The classroom had been completely trashed. There were several desks upturned, a computer on the floor, papers scattered everywhere. The only sound was the spinning of the black industrial fan sitting on an old beat up, musty brown office chair with broken wheels. I nearly tripped on the black and orange extension cord that powered the fan as I came into the room. I looked at my watch, 12:15. Time for lunch. Significant incidents almost always increased during lunch time. It was one of the few times of the day when all the students passed by one another in route to the cafeteria, providing plenty of opportunities for antagonizing one another by throwing out insults to open up old wounds and push each other's buttons. Kenny was a muscular teenager who hit puberty at an early age. He was strong and well-coordinated. Resembling more of a professional wrestler in his ludicrous outfits, cut off jean shorts, mullet style, shoulder length dirty blond hair, and white t-shirt that was two sizes too small.

I greeted the students warmly as they got off the bus each morning; I tried to establish positive rapport for the day and put them in a friendly state of mind. Deputy Richards would stand on guard next to me, contrasting the exact opposite of what I was trying to convey. He would consume his morning protein shake and carelessly rattle off about dishing out "dirt sandwich" to the students if they stepped out of line. The school resource officers were on rotating shifts, planted at Bishop for periodic durations of six to twelve months, then they were replaced irrespective of their performance. We never knew what personality type we would get when a new officer was assigned; some were male officers, some female, some short tempered, some with patience, some tolerated their placement better than others, some needed almost the entire duration of their assignment to become acclimated to our unique school, some never did. It all came down to his or her personality type and experience. This made collaborating with police officers difficult sometimes; they didn't always agree with our mission.

Deputy Richards, for instance, absolutely hated to be challenged. Unfortunately, he was horribly misplaced for someone who couldn't tolerate disrespect. It pained him unforgivingly to stand by and watch one of the students disrupt school campus, but Bishop wasn't like most schools, it was its own animal entirely. Deputy Richards' reputation was preceded only by his temper, which was equal to, or worse than most of our students at Bishop, only heightening the tension throughout the day. Like many deputies before him, he had been reassigned to Bishop unwillingly. It may have been an arbitrary placement, it may have been because he needed further training, but most of us speculated he was placed there by his supervisor as punishment because he needed to learn how to cool his temper. An ex-marine, he was a towering 6 foot 4 inches and approximately 230 pounds packed full of solid muscle. "Who do I need to make famous today?" he would say. He was an alchemist of machoism and testosterone. This is part of what made Bishop School unconventional. It was famous for bringing together all sorts of people from different walks of life, throwing them in a melting pot and seeing what happens.

Having a police officer available was a mixed blessing. Unquestionably, there were times when a student's behavior exceeded the capabilities and resources of the staff. Had a police officer not been nearby, one of us would be severely hurt trying to restrain a student. Many of the teachers employed by Bishop were aged, female staff, certainly a physical mismatch for a rage-filled teenager hurling chairs across the classroom. Other times, students who were more fearful of the law, were de-escalated merely by Deputy Richards stepping out of his office and silently announcing his presence. These students would quickly get their act together, suddenly following the same directions from a teacher they defied just moments before, fearful of the Deputy's wrath. Yet the sword cut both ways. The presence of strength also breeds competition. Some Bishop students had numerous run-ins with the law on the streets, and were raised by their parents, peers, and community to distrust law enforcement. Deputy Richards' thousand yard stare and power walk did little to deter their ill-fated decisions. If anything, his macho persona was irresistible to the students. He was an immovable object and they were the unstoppable force--a match made in heaven. If he had his way, all students would be conducting themselves in boot camp fashion, doing push-ups and running a mile for every infraction they committed. From Deputy Richard's first day at Bishop, he received an unwelcome attitude from Kenny, which ignited a rivalry that only blossomed with time. Every day, Deputy Richards hoped for a good reason to throw Kenny in the back of his police cruiser and haul him off to jail.

Kenny stood poised before Deputy Richards; rather than quivering with fear, he invited the challenge. Inside the room they stared at one another with rage burning through their eyes.

Due to the rehabilitative nature of Bishop School, you had to be a repeat offender to get the handcuffs, and even then, you weren't guaranteed to be charged with anything. Kenny had destroyed classrooms before, and recently he hadn't been doing himself any favors in terms of avoiding arrest. Most of the time, Kenny was quiet and kept to himself. He did, however, ruminate on his fixation with aliens, an unhealthy and sometimes detrimental obsession. It wasn't uncommon for Kenny to speak very fervently on the matter. The aliens, or "body snatchers" as he would sometimes call them, referencing his favorite movie on the subject, were always out to get him. "Mr. Clark, I've got some unreal data on area 51 that you won't believe," he would say.

"Looking forward to it," I would cautiously say, always intrigued by his passion and thirst for more knowledge, but not always game to venture down that particular path with him. I hadn't yet decided whether it was healthy to feed in to his fixation. "Yep, body snatchers have abducted 10 more people but they don't know they've been abducted so they just keep going on with their life," he would say spookily as his eyes grew wider. Kenny spoke with such conviction he had me second-guessing my own reality.

Aliens aside, when he got angry, he took the whole world down with him. When the nurse called for Kenny to take his daily dose of antipsychotics, he had apparently refused. Because of Deputy Richard's temper, we used him sparingly, as a last resort to control the chaos before it escalated beyond our capabilities. Unless it was absolutely necessary to their safety, we didn't try to physically manage students Kenny's age; high schoolers posed too much of a threat to someone's safety because of their size.

Kenny had been diagnosed with multiple conditions including autism and oppositional defiant disorder, among others, and was suspected to suffer from schizophrenia, though he was slightly too young to be diagnosed. He had been treated by more than ten psychiatrists in his life, and we couldn't keep up with all of the conflicting diagnoses assigned to him. They didn't make much sense at this point. Some staff resolved to identify his condition as "messed up," as that was much easier to wrap their head around. Kenny was unwavering; once he saw red, he would challenge King Kong himself to a fight if given the opportunity. I could personally testify to Kenny's relentless temper over the years. I lost track of how many times I saw him put in pain compliance positions by different officers. The irony of his temper was merciless. He would find himself completely restrained and incapable of movement, just long enough for the officer to think he settled the confrontation. But much to the officer's disbelief, Kenny would light up one more time and mouth off, "When I get out of the handcuffs I'm gonna kick your fuckin ass!" This made Kenny insufferable for police officers with sensitive egos, because he never gave any authority figure any satisfaction.

"You're soft as cotton, boy!" Shouted Deputy Richards. "I see you cutting me that eye, boy, you wanna eat the dirt?"

"I dare you to try it!" Kenny shouted defiantly, his croaky southern twang ricocheting off the walls.

"Kenny, last warning, you walk your ass up to the nurses office and take your medicine or I'm gonna drag you out of this classroom head first boy!" fired the Deputy.

"How can I go there with you? I have too many other places to be." Kenny said mysteriously. "Besides, the doctors are trying to kill me with these fucking pills. They set my brain on fire!" he belabored.

"Kenny, what are you saying?" I interjected. "You aren't thinking clearly, look at your choices, look what you did to the room. You're not acting like yourself."

"I know what you all want from me, you want to turn my brains into stew! You can't have *my* brain! Just keep on searching!" he said.

Trying to encourage Kenny to make a good choice, I used a relaxing voice, in an effort to diffuse the tension between him and the Deputy. "Come on Kenny, chill out, walk up to the office. We will call your parents, you go home suspended for the day. Doesn't that sound a little better, rather than going to jail?" Kenny loosened, he began to give himself some breathing space, considering my recommendation.

"And you *are* on your way to jail, Kenny, if you don't get your head straight in the next ten seconds, you're gonna get a nice view of the town from the window in my backseat!" *Deputy ruined it.*

Kenny returned fire, flipping his mullet-like hair from side to side, his country accent augmented now, "Why should I? You people don't listen to a shit fucking word I say, bro!"

Kenny strictly addressed Deputy Richards now, as he geared up for another round of insults, "Look at you standing there in your green suit, think you're all fancy, coming after my brain. I got security on me." Kenny flipped his mullet to the side of his shoulder, raised both arms and flexed them towards his head. Pointing to each bicep, he said, "This here is Tango and Cash, and they don't very much like you!" Kenny puffed out his cheeks, and bowed up his chest in rebellion. Deputy Richards braced himself, started closing the distance between himself and Kenny, his tall frame hovering over the confused teenager, signaling that at any moment he was going to snap, and Kenny would be face down on the floor. His voice came out menacing and threatening, "Kenny you're a peacock, you're showing your feathers but you can't fly boy."

"Oh you wanna watch me fly mother fucker…?" said, Kenny.

I cut in again before Deputy Richards could get a chance to speak. "Kenny, we all know Tango and Cash mean serious business. We don't want to upset them any further." Humor was my way of getting Kenny to cooperate, I'd play in to his little fantasy until he got his medicine, which was my goal for him. But Deputy Richards gave me a sideways look, he was seething, clearly not in agreement with my approach. His goal was to take Kenny to jail. I continued, "You have every right to protect your brain, and we wouldn't dare try to get past your security, which is clearly too tough for us. If you reconsider taking your medicine, you will probably feel better. Tango and Cash will feel better too." Kenny took a step back from the Deputy. "OK, Clark. I think I can trust you," Kenny said carefully. "You guys shoulda just been honest with me in the first place."

This was a win in my book, but Deputy Richards was still reluctant to forego his ego.

"Hey Kenny," he said, as Kenny turned to walk out the door with me. "Dare you to fly..."

"AHHH! AHHH!" cried Kenny, before abruptly spinning around to face Deputy Richards with an austere look about him.

"Hey Deputy Richards, fuck...you! Come get me!" And with that, he sprinted off towards the exit of the school campus. Because Bishop was a forgotten school, we operated on a very low budget, not even enough to afford a fence that encompassed the entire campus. Once Kenny became unhinged, he was an immediate safety threat to himself and others. Kenny now took precedence over anything else that was happening at that time. Moreover, there was the risk that the school would be held liable for any harm that came to Kenny while he was off campus. He had to be stopped as soon as possible.

"Can__ some_ come_ ing 8." Mr. Smith's timing was horrible as always, again he found himself asking for someone to come to building 8, no one knowing why.

I immediately reprimanded him, "Now is not the time Mr. Smith!"

Deputy Richards was already in his car, peeling out of the school exit with his lights on and adrenaline pumping. Fast forward to several minutes later and I found myself pursuing Kenny across dirt roads, questioning my job, my life, my purpose here. The setting offered little favors in these runaway situations. The surrounding area that encompassed the school was broken up into a neighborhood thick with run-down homes, loose dogs, gun toting residents, and dense, wooded areas with trees that stretched for hundreds of yards. I leapt over a fence, completely disregarding the "beware of dog" signs that were posted, and pulled spider webs off of my face. I was chasing the small dot up ahead that was Kenny. *Just follow the dot*. I had blood running down my arm, probably a thorn bush. Every step Kenny took I took as well. My heart was pounding, I was sure at any minute either Kenny or I would be looking at the barrel of a defensive homeowner or be dragged to the ground by a protective watchdog. In the midst of Kenny's instability, he could just as easily run himself into a stranger's house, right into a scared homeowner's handgun; or throw himself into oncoming traffic, fleeing the aliens he thought were pursuing him. When Kenny would experience psychosis, his perception of reality was skewed. He could have very well convinced himself he was running from the FBI, who wanted to surgically extract parts of his brain in order to fight off the impending threat of aliens. My reality, on the other hand, was very real. I needed to stop Kenny right now.

"Ahead on the left!" I radioed to Deputy Richards, trying to catch my breath as he raced through the nearby neighborhoods in pursuit.

"Cut him off!" he replied.

"I'm trying!"

"I have him dead ahead."

160

While sprinting, I would occasionally look over through a myriad of trees and see flashes of red and blue police lights zipping down the back roads that intersected one another.

"Where are you? I can't find you!"

"Over here. Do you see me?"

"Just barely!"

"He turned, I lost him."

"Where is he?"

"No idea!"

"Wait, I think I see him."

"Can you hear me? Is my walkie-talkie still working or am I out of range?"

"Hello?"

Seconds passed.

"I can hear you, what's your 20 now?"

"Just ahead on the right, can you see him?"

I caught a flash of Kenny's mullet as he looped a corner and wrestled with a thorn bush, middle fingers in the air.

"I got him just ahead, he is flipping me off as he runs."

Have I been temporarily deputized? I thought.

Checklist item number twelve: chasing paranoid high school student through the woods with a police officer. Again, something that wasn't in the job description. *Is this my life?* I hopped a fence and clamored for freedom as a loose metal piece of fencing tore down my stomach and left a hole in my shirt. I feared for Kenny and what would happen to him if he wasn't caught soon. I could tell from his desperate body language, zigzagging through the trees and running across neighborhood roads without looking, that his demented thoughts had taken over and he was starting to slip into psychosis.

***

I must get away! I must get away! The big green angry alien is chasing me! If I can get far enough away they won't take me.

AHH! Why do they still follow me? I'll hurt them, I'll hurt them so bad!

The green alien drives his ship with blinding lights flashing red and blue, the regular jumps fences behind me.

The green alien is mean, he wants my brain, he wants to dissect my brain!

I must stop them.

I know what I must do…

***

Kenny looked back at me in angst, he wasn't even tired yet. There was roughly 30 yards between us when he suddenly stopped in midstride. Just like that, he stopped dead in his tracks. *What does this mean?* He eerily walked himself to the side of the road, and crouched down in a row of green bushes. *Was he hiding? Surely he knows I watched him go under there.* I paused to see what he would do. His behavior was so peculiarly sinister, did I really want to find out?

163

Everything grew forebodingly quiet, until all that could be heard was the panting from my breath.

"Deputy Richards…" I whispered, too suspicious to speak above a whisper.

"Come in, what's your 20?"

"We're stopped…just ahead off First street. I'm not sure what's going through his head, but he's behaving very bizarre."

"I got him, I'm closing in, gonna shut him down," he said over the walkie-talkie, and his police lights came from around the corner.

Deputy Richards pulled the front of his cruiser up to the edge of the street where the asphalt met the grass leading to the bushes that revealed Kenny's whereabouts. The top of Kenny's forehead peered over the highest rows of thorns. With the cruiser in park position, the Deputy stepped out slowly yet purposefully, in a militaristic fashion. Kenny slowly rose from a crouched position and emerged from the green bushes as if he had undergone some sort of diabolical metamorphosis. I began walking towards the two of them unsteadily. It was a western stare down. As much as Deputy Richards had been through in his combat experience, nothing could've prepared him for what was about to happen.

"HOORAWWWWRRRRR!!!" HOORAWWWWRRRRR!!!"

There was a penetrating discord of incomprehensible pandemonium coming from Kenny that was out of body foreign shrieks and shrills, consistent with what one would expect to hear during an demonic exorcism.

"HOORAWWWWRRRRR!!!" HOORAWWWWRRRRR!!!" Kenny was raising the dead. The volume of his screaming was offensive. I covered my ears, a reflexive reaction to the discomfort I felt as I watched him change.

"HOORAWWWWRRRRR!!!" HOORAWWWWRRRRR!!!" Kenny prepared his attack, taking the stance of a gorilla, and pointed towards the big green alien he lined up in his sights.

With a disembodied voice, he targeted Deputy Richards, "KILL THE ALIENS!" he screamed, with his fist pumping through the air. "KILL THE ALIENS!"

Deputy Richards called Kenny's bluff. Big mistake. Kenny launched his body forward and charged angrily towards Deputy Richard's car. He moved with catlike reflexes. At a distance of 6 feet from the police cruiser, he leapt nimbly on top of the parked police car, where he planted both feet. Deputy Richards was so caught off guard he stood frozen in shock and horror. Kenny landed on the hood of the car and used it as a platform to bounce back into the air in one swift movement, maximizing efficiency and wasting not even a millisecond. Now airborne again, he outstretched both feet and took the shape of someone who was going down a water slide flat on his back. There was a loud thud. Kenny had leapt from the ground, onto the hood of the police car as a launch pad, and flew through the air, dropkicking Deputy Richards square in the chest and sending him sprawling backwards. The sheer force and perfectly timed trajectory of Kenny's kick had sent the deputy into a complete backflip as he tumbled onto the asphalt in the middle of the street behind him. His favorite pair of sunglasses had been smashed under his own weight. Kenny was rage.

"HOLY SHIT!" I said aloud to myself, downright shocked and admittedly amused. No sooner did I realize what I had said aloud did I begin sprinting towards the impromptu battle arena to check on Deputy Richards. My ongoing concern for Kenny had now shifted to the Deputy, where I least expected my sympathy to land. *I don't know if I can take much more drama today.* The Deputy, normally exuding the utmost confidence and supreme discipline, was mortified. He sighed and moaned in pain, trying to process the situation. He picked his head up, feeling around for his weapons on his belt to make sure he hadn't lost any of them from the impact. Embarrassed and enraged, Deputy Richards picked his head up off the street, only to find Kenny now running back in the direction of campus, navigating his way once again through the trees, convinced that he was still running for his life.

Deputy Richards stood upright, recovering from the blow, foot imprints from Kenny's size 11 shoes marked his chest. With asphalt gravel embedded in his forearm from the assault, he dusted himself off, stared down at Kenny who was picking up speed, and shouted, "I'm gonna make you famous!"

"You'll never catch me!" screamed Kenny, not even bothering to turn around.

The chase was on again.

***

Back on campus, a green lizard dangled from Trevor's fingers. He recovered from my negligent quarterbacking skills by now and was skipping class to participate in his favorite pastime, nature hunting. Trevor rolled in the grass, laughing and frolicking with his newfound friend, who was very unhappy to have been disturbed. Mrs. Jones, again, was at the rescue, cajoling a jaunty Trevor back to class.

"Trevor, drop the lizard and get to class," she said in her motherly tone, slightly annoyed at having found him skipping class for the same reason, yet again. "You are so smart and creative, think about how well you can do on your school projects. If you love nature so much maybe this is something you can write about in your English class?" she suggested, trying to redirect his creative energy into something academically productive.

"Don't disturb me, you're gonna make me drop him!" his squeaky voice echoed, as he returned to hanging the lizard upside down by its tail. Trevor rolled on the ground, his blue jeans covered in grass stains, matching his famous, oversized white tennis shoes that you could spot a mile away. His shoes were famous around campus because they resembled astronaut boots. It was as if he happened across a pair of shoes that were three sizes too big but resolved to wear them anyway, assuming he would grow into them at some point.

"Trevor, this is hardly a reason for you to be out of class. You need to stand up, put the lizard down, and get back to your room before I call your mother and send you home. I've already given you several warnings, you know you can do better than this." Trevor's face was disgruntled at Mrs. Jones's intrusion. He snorted as he tried to contain the lizard which scrambled around Trevor's fingers and bent its body in half.

"He peed on me!" cried Trevor, his whiney voice even more pronounced now. "You stupid little fucker!" he shouted out insolently, suddenly the most hapless child in the world. Trevor, distracted, had begun to accidentally lose his grip on the lizard, who felt it was time to break free. The lizard, now tasting freedom, scurried through the abnormally tall blades of bright green grass in a getaway attempt.

"Wait, I didn't mean that. I'm sorry, I take it back!" Trevor called after the lizard, clamoring for forgiveness as he frantically crawled on all fours to recapture his reluctant friend. The lizard wouldn't be afforded an opportunity to reconsider Trevor's request, as his insides were splattered across the ground by the foot of someone in a massive hurry. Trevor was left to suffer his loss and tried to piece together the moment. It was a blur, he saw only a flash of cut off jean shorts and a white t-shirt, and heard only the sounds of someone screaming in mental agony. But alas, he spotted the distinguishable trademark mullet that defined only one student on campus. "Damn you, Kenny!" He shouted, as he raised his hands to the sky.

Trevor pointed in the direction of the runner, and scrunched up his nose in disbelief, "Mrs. Jones, that asshole just killed my only friend!"

"Trevor, you get to class and come to my office later to talk about the lizard!" Mrs. Jones became suddenly aware of the urgency in getting Trevor to safety, as Kenny was on the loose and unpredictable. She ushered Trevor off to his room, and immediately after, a police car roared just outside the entrance of the school, being driven by a very angry Deputy.

***

I fell into a burnin' ring of fire,

I went down, down, down

And the flames went higher

And it burns, burns, burns

The ring of fire, the ring of fire

Johnny Cash was singing to me through the radio station inside the police car, summing up the moment in its entirety. I sat feeling like I was on a roller coaster, Deputy Richards was maneuvering the cruiser deftly as we

171

whipped around the curves in the road and ramped over sidewalks. I had always wanted to drive a cop car, I imagined this was the closest I would get. I reflected on everything that I had just witnessed, but not wanting to further damage Deputy Richards's pride, I kept my mouth shut. Nothing needed to be said, yet the lack of conversation between us said it all. I felt as if he could hear my thoughts as he kept staring at me through his peripheral vision, probably wondering when I was going to laugh and whether he could restrain himself from lashing out at me if I did. In truth, I didn't know what to feel. I was actually rather impressed with Kenny's display of acrobatics. I wanted to talk about it right away. I thought about sticking an imaginary microphone in the Deputy's face and saying, "How are you feeling right now?" Maybe that would generate some laughter, but Deputy Richards clearly wasn't up for conversation at the time, especially not at his own expense.

The car sped into Deputy Richards's reserved parking spot, and as he slammed on the brakes a screeching noise erupted from the car tires. Just then a large triangular shaped rock the size of a human head flew over the windshield and bounced off the front office wall. Kenny's crisis state of mind hadn't abated. We were close enough now to pick up service on our walkie-talkies again. Mr. Williams was the hawk that saw everything from his front office window, "All teachers get your students inside immediately and lock the doors," he urged over the air.

And it burns, burns, burns,

The ring of fire, the ring of fire

***

That rock simply won't do. The next one will find its mark.

The aliens are coming after me. They look at me with their laser eyes.

If only I can get back home, I can hide from these body snatchers in my TV screen.

This rock will smash the aliens head in, this one will certainly do the trick. I will steal his spaceship and teleport back to my TV screen.

173

***

Deputy Richards was now my human shield. I stood behind the frame of his body, unsure of what to do next. He, on the other hand, knew exactly what it would come down to in order to stop Kenny, who was gathering more ammo to throw at us.

"Kenny, if you turn that rock loose I'm gonna zap you." It wasn't a threat, it was a promise. We hesitantly closed in on Kenny, who was still dead set on causing massive bodily harm with rocks big enough to cave in our heads and dismember out facial features. If any of these rocks landed it would surely mean reconstructive surgery. Kenny arched his arm back as a pitcher would just before he released a 95mph fastball. I screamed, Kenny screamed, the Deputy screamed. I heard a sharp, vibrant crackling noise slice through the air like a firework that was immediately followed by a thunderous thud. Kenny dropped the rock and tumbled several feet away, both arms went limp and hung by his side as his body stiffened up, his muscles impaired and rendered utterly useless.

"Hey guys, I think my radio is broken," a nasally voice behind me echoed. Mr. Smith, aloof as ever, had been ignorant of the teeming chaos that had overtaken the school. The Deputy and I stood drenched in sweat, catching our breath, my shirt torn from jumping a fence, exasperated by our ordeal, and were now acutely vexed by Mr. Smith's attempt to layer his trivial problems upon us at a most inopportune time. His staggering inattention, superimposed onto the madness that had just swarmed the school, was too much for me to absorb. Clearly, Kenny stretched out on the grass was of no immediate concern to him.

Together Deputy Richards and I collectively shouted, "WHAT DO YOU WANT?"

"Our toilet is backed up in building 8." he said, "I've been trying to tell somebody all day."

We scoffed and shared a look of infuriation and turned our back on Mr. Smith, as if we just realized he was a figment of our imagination. As expected, Mr. Smith faded quietly away and went about his business.

Kenny had been hit with 50,000 volts of electricity from Deputy Richards's Taser. His languid body now lay quietly on the ground, incapacitated. The Deputy would later consider charging him with assault with a deadly weapon due to the size of the rocks and his intent on bludgeoning us to death, but would eventually concede that a 72 hour hold in the psychiatric unit was more appropriate for the time being. The Taser barbs in his chest now a part of Kenny's shirt, he gazed up at the sky listlessly. Kenny had taken us on a high speed chase through the surrounding neighborhood, twice attacked an officer of the law, endangered his own life, and vandalized school property all because he missed his medication. For the first time in 30 minutes of unadulterated rage, he now lay completely still and quiet. He calmly took deep breaths, as if the Taser had yanked him right out of his psychosis.

Above him, Deputy Richards stood and stared down at him menacingly, whispering, "I told you I'd make you famous boy..."

Chapter 7

Me and Mrs. Jones

It is astounding how quickly the students and staff were able to bounce back from these strange occurrences. How many kids go to school and see a friend tasered by a police officer? Then again, perhaps these events came to pass with such frequency that they weren't so strange at all. Time slipped away as usual. I hadn't had any time to reward myself with lunch for my hard work. The next inevitable crisis was soon to occur. I couldn't behave as if I had time to sit down and eat, who was I kidding?

I strode through the office hallway, fighting the urge to steal a half-eaten sandwich someone had left on a desk. In an adjacent room, I heard the sounds of a teenage voice screaming in protest, shortly followed by a determined sounding "Don't you dare!" "Don't you dare!" "Don't you dare do this to me!" I read once that a shark's sense of smell was so impressive, it could detect one drop of blood in a million drops of water. Much like the shark, I could identify this distressed voice amongst

177

millions of people. It was Duncan. I wrapped myself around the corner of the wall that failed to entrap the noise from Duncan's protesting. I peeked my head through the doorway and glanced inside.

Duncan looked like what most would imagine a stereotypical person pulled straight off the streets of Ireland would resemble. He was fair skinned, with fiery red curly hair, and thousands of freckles on his face, one for each curse word he used a day. He turned to look at me with fierce, bloodshot eyes. He was roughly thirteen, socially awkward, and unusually dressed, though fashion wasn't in at Bishop. Duncan preferred grey basketball shorts two sizes too small to fit his portly outline. Only the bottom trim of the shorts were visible, shielded by his untucked white collared shirt that hung past his knees. Where his shirt ended, his socks began. They ran their way down his legs to his off-white, faded Nike basketball shoes that would never step foot on a basketball court. Duncan's disability manifested in an intense, almost unmanageable fixation on the internet. Duncan's behavior problems didn't take long to sum up--when the internet worked, he was happy as a clam. When the internet went down, all hell broke loose. One of the reasons he was sent to Bishop was that his dependence on media stimulation became so overwhelming it created major disruptions in his previous school, resulting in sometimes violent, tantrum behavior and screaming that could last for hours. Upon first glance, one would never suspect Duncan of being anything short of an innocent, harmless boy. In about ninety percent of interactions with him, he seemed a cuddly redheaded koala. He appeared to be the type of kid that received unsolicited hugs from strangers for being too cute. Yet when denied access to his favorite cartoon clips online, he would take on the behavior of an irate, potty-mouthed drunken sailor. Ostensibly, the internet had crashed and Duncan was not having it. This was one of the many times the internet server went down, so nothing could be done for him except to wait out the problem.

"Duncan, how ya doing there buddy?" I asked. He sat in a chair, hunched over, sweating bullets, with both hands on opposite sides of the computer monitor. He stared furiously into the computer screen as if awaiting a secret message that was long overdue.

"Duncan..." I said again. "Are you okay?"

Duncan painfully peeled his eyes away from the computer screen. It tortured him to turn away. He looked at me with his pale white jaw clenched, and began convulsing. The collar on his shirt twisted and stretched beyond its stitching. Then this incredibly sweet, innocent looking boy spoke to me directly, "Mr. Clark. The...Fucking...Internet....Is...Not....Fucking...Working ...Okay? You think I have time to answer your questions you jerk? Talk to the hand!" Duncan raised the palm of his right hand to face me, as if he retained some mystical power to prevent me from talking any further. He was a ticking time bomb. I noticed an upturned trash can on the floor with debris thrown about the room and referred to it disappointedly, "Duncan, did you do this to the trash can?"

"Well yes, of course I did," he replied curtly. "Why? Because the internet is not working you asshole! Fix this internet now you piece of shit! Fix this internet!"

"Whoa...do you think that is going to get the internet working, pal?" Duncan began punching the computer screen at the sound of my voice.

"Hey! You do not mistreat these computers or you will not use them, whether the internet works or not. You know better than that," said Mr. Morales, sitting on the opposite side of the room.

I nodded towards Mr. Morales as if to say, "You good here?" He nodded in return and gave me the thumbs up. Realizing I was doing more harm than good, I turned to continue making my way down the hallway. I was stopped dead in my tracks at the sound of Duncan screaming, "Goodbye dickhead!" Duncan was never short on creativity, never using the same insult twice. I struggled to swallow my laughter, and somewhat begrudgingly, carried on until my feet led me to the sound of hushed crying, just outside the best decorated office there was. I glanced inside this room to see the walls were garnished with pictures of children, artwork from the students, thoughtful cards and words of inspiration such as, "Beauty catches the attention but character catches the heart," or, "So often you find that the students you're trying to inspire are the ones that end up inspiring you," and even, "A great teacher takes a hand, opens a mind, and touches a heart," amongst others.

After all was said and done, Mrs. Jones was one of the students' favorite staff. Now a school administrator, Mrs. Jones's love and previous experience teaching special education children made it such that her heart never left the classroom. When not in her office, she would often float about campus showering unsuspecting students with gifts of chocolate, balloons, and stickers, gracing them with her sweet presence. Despite her lavish gifts, it was her kindness and words of wisdom that found their way to the students' hearts. Perhaps this relationship between her and the students came to be because qualities such as love, support, and motherly nurturing were all characteristics absent in many of the students' biological mothers.

In spite of Mrs. Jones's angelic disposition, something was bringing her down. Outside her door, I heard the continued soft sobbing, as if she was trying to not be heard. I wasn't sure if I should intrude, but *maybe I could lend her my ear for a few minutes and cheer her up?* I thought. After all, her door wasn't completely shut, maybe it was a subtle invitation for comfort.

(Tap tap), I quietly knocked on the door, only loud enough for her to hear.

"*Just a second*," a shaky voice called out.

I immediately felt as if I had made the wrong decision to knock. "I can come back, no problem," I said. As I turned to walk away, the door softly opened, and a teary-eyed face emerged around the corner like a sad raccoon. Mrs. Jones's black hair draped around her shoulders. She tried to disguise her tears and turned her face into a somber smile. "Come on in," she said weakly.

"Sure, okay," I said. "Mind if I grab a chair?"

"Of course, help yourself."

Once inside her office, I was swallowed by the artwork. To my left hung a corkboard where children's lime green and sky blue artwork popped out of the walls to greet me. Despite the décor, I wasn't overwhelmed. I began to understand why students enjoyed sitting in Mrs. Jones's office. I began to develop an appreciation for the coziness of the space, and despite being initially regretful for involving myself, found that I was beginning to feel rather comforted. Next to me, sat a box of tissues on a paper covered desk. The box seemed to be out of reach for Mrs. Jones, who now took her seat in front of her computer on the other side of the office. As wonderful as Mrs. Jones was, she wasn't known for her organization. The desk in her office was drowning under the weight of miscellaneous papers, the same ones that were always there. Seeing that she was holding back more tears, I pulled one tissue from the box and extended my arm to her, signaling politely for her to take it from me.

Mrs. Jones smiled and graciously took the tissue from me. She fidgeted with her hands and interlaced her fingers across her lap, as if she had been sent to the principal's office for misbehavior. She caught the tear that began to roll down her cheek and wiped it away to the side of her face.

"I'm embarrassed," she said. "I usually wait until I get in my car to do my crying." Feelings of sympathy grew, I had never seen Mrs. Jones truly upset. As much as I wanted to take her pain away, *I need to be careful not to overreach*, I thought to myself. A brief moment of consideration passed, and I decided I would just move forward like I would with anyone else--keep it simple and offer my support.

"If you don't mind me asking, are you okay?" I asked supportively.

"I wouldn't want to bore you with the details," she said. "How's that beautiful girlfriend of yours?"

"She's great, but she would be upset with me if I let you change the subject so quickly."

Mrs. Jones laughed briefly, and for a second I thought my work there was all done. Then she remembered she was sad. "She's trained you well," she said morosely.

I half-smiled, "If you want to talk about it, I'm all ears."

"Well, let's put it this way, at least I'm going to have more time to myself now, no one to fuss at me about doing the dishes." Mrs. Jones was using gallows humor to shield her insecurities. Her mascara was now running and as she lifted the tissue to wipe her eyes, I noticed a tan line on her finger incongruent with the rest of her skin. *Her*

185

wedding ring is gone, I thought. My heart sank. This was a topic that was out of my field of expertise. Part of me wanted to run and swap places with the nearest female staff member, possibly a more suitable conversational partner.

Mrs. Jones gauged my reaction as I furrowed my eyebrows, the room suddenly growing warm. I had put the pieces together--her downtrodden look this morning when she intercepted Trevor, the crying behind her door, and the missing wedding ring. Mrs. Jones suffered from a heartache, and she had a big heart, which meant a lot of pain. *Then who sent her the flowers I noticed earlier?* I didn't know exactly what to say, I hated to see such a nice person look so melancholy. She didn't deserve it. I had hoped for some brilliant words of wisdom to suddenly enter my mind, allowing me to free Mrs. Jones from her burdens. All I could muster was a point of validation, "I'm sorry. I can't imagine how hard that must be."

She lifted her head momentarily and forced the beginning of a smile, as if to show appreciation for my concern.

"I've done this before though, you know."

"You mean…"

"This is my second time around. I can't hang on to a marriage." She said, laughing bitterly.

"I'm sure that doesn't make it any easier," I said, handing her another tissue.

"No, it makes it worse in a way, because I thought I was done," she said, with only her eyes rising over the top of the mountain of tissues balled up between her hands and face.

"I feel like a failure," she said, with a vacant expression on her face.

"You shouldn't feel that way. These kids here, they love you. I don't know what they would do without you."

"It's ironic you say that. Because I can't fix them," she said as a matter of fact. "And that's what keeps me up most nights. Charlie used to say it was ruining our marriage, I never believed him, and then it ended. Now John says the same thing. He always argues with me, he says, "You need to leave your job and get a normal one, no one's gonna fix those kids, you've been trying for years and every day you come home with new bruises and new scratches. You're a great big ball of stress. It's like you're not even here. Do I even exist? You really think those kids are worth it?"

Mrs. Jones continued, "It's a trend across both my marriages, I now realize. I pour my heart and soul into this job, these kids are my life, and when I get home, I have nothing left to give. Zero energy. There is no ounce of me I have left for my family, and now I'm ruined. Sometimes I fear for these students here. I fear for Chad, for Kenny, for Trevor, for Eddie, for Matthew, for Zack, for all of them, and all the kids around the world just like them. I ask myself, are we really making a difference? What is all of this for? Why do I come to work to get beat up? Just the other day I was punched in the face trying to break up a fight. Did I sign up to get punched in the face? No. I mean what are we doing here? Hm? Just what exactly are we doing?" Her voice had started to escalate and my concern for her grew.

I was speechless. This was a microcosm of a much larger issue. Not only was Bishop the forgotten school, the students the forgotten students, but the staff were forgotten as well. No one ever told us we were doing a great job, we just had to believe in what we were doing, while our work lives took its toll on our own mental health, and our own family's happiness. Truly, most people are not cut out to work at a place like this. We idealize growth and change. At times, we go many days, weeks, or months, seeing little, if any improvement in the students. *What do we rely on?* Between a child's parents, community, culture, and environment, there are so many uncontrollable variables. The strength the faculty found in one another came to be the bonds formed to get us through the day. You can't go home and explain how your day was and expect someone to fully understand. You just have to live it and breathe it. You have to feel the sweat pouring down your face as you're chasing a scared runaway student through traffic in the nearby neighborhoods, you have to bounce back from spit in your eye, rocks thrown at your head, and being called every vitriolic name in the book, all because you are someone who wants to make a difference. A noble cause and often thankless job, garnering little sympathy or understanding from outsiders. Most people wouldn't last ten seconds on Bishop's campus before quitting.

I was still somewhat new to the world of Bishop, not too long out of college, never been married, and never tried to work this job on top of balancing a family. *Maybe the only reason I can manage it is because I've haven't gotten that far in life? Should I be concerned about my future? This job had torn apart two marriages with Mrs. Jones, who was undoubtedly one of the sweetest people in the world. Maybe I didn't realize what I had gotten myself into.*

I thought of something my dad would have said, about how "teachers are overworked and underappreciated." I couldn't agree more. This wasn't the Mrs. Jones I was first introduced to. The Mrs. Jones I came to enjoy was someone who would perk herself up with the right touch of coffee and choice of music. At least once a week, I would find myself sitting down in my office, in a rare moment of calm. Maybe I'm wiping grits off my clothes, or maybe I'm nursing a slap in the face. But just across the hallway, the soulful voice of the classic rhythm and blues singer, Billy Paul, can be heard singing the song that launched him into fame, "Me and Mrs. Jones." Mrs. Jones, being a naturally skilled singer and leader in her church choir, would join in from her office, complementing the original recording suitably. The effect was contagious. Mr. Williams, who sat at the main entrance of the building, would set down the phone in his hand after placing the caller on hold, confirm that all intercom switches were turned off, and using his baritone voice, join in somewhere along the second verse, usually standing atop his chair, "Holding hands, making all kinds of plans, while the jukebox plays our favorite song." The two would sing together in harmony, their voices rebounding off the cheap wooden walls throughout the hallway. The trail their voices left would find my ear, and I would join shortly thereafter with Mr. Morales, and any surrounding staff fortunate to be walking through the office at the time. Our walkie-talkies became makeshift microphones, all singing gregariously in discordance, all obnoxiously hitting separate notes like a musician's worse nightmare, "But it's much too strong to let it cool down now." "Now she'll go her way and I'll go mine." By the end of the song, there would be a group of adults

191

dancing suavely down the hallway, sharing the stage with one another, passing our "microphones" back and forth for each to demonstrate his or her solo abilities. Mrs. Jones, being the most talented of all of us, arguably the only one who should be singing publicly, would carry her soprano notes the highest, letting her voice smoothly carry over and escalate, and then quiet again in sync with the original track. "Me and Mrs. Jones, Mrs. Jones, Mrs. Jones." And that was how powerfully her personality could influence us to drop what we are doing, and put a smile on our face, and not take life too seriously. *I guess we all have to be a little quirky to do this job*, I thought. So to see Mrs. Jones now, in this emotionally crumbled, deteriorated state, was hard to swallow. It was the slow, mental, wearing down of her good intentions, which were only periodically reinforced by small results. The only progress from the students was made in baby steps. Watching them improve, relapse, improve again, then relapse again, was slowly breaking her heart.

"What made you want to do this in the first place?" I said, hoping this would lead her to achieve some sort of tranquility, even if only for a moment.

"Well, of course I love kids, I love to teach, but as cliché as it sounds…I just wanted to put a smile on a child's face, and hopefully a child would put a smile on mine as well."

"I think that is important," I replied. "I have people misinterpret what I do here every day. You know, all my life I caught myself wanting to solve more problems for people than I can. Inside Bishop, only *we* know what we were doing, only *we* know it is something meaningful. Usually, I fight back feelings of insecurity with the sarcastic comments friends or acquaintances make when they refer to my job. People say to me, 'Off to save the world again today?' 'Going to do your guidance counselor thing?' The latter comment infuriates me, because it is such a gross misrepresentation of what I do. I hear their voices in my head sometimes, and I feel a little sting in my chest. It's like a constant reminder that so few people appreciate our goals here. Outside of Bishop, my job as a behavior analyst is met with perpetual misunderstanding and casual mockery. If I had a nickel for every derisive comment about the futility or meaninglessness behind working at a place such as this, I would be a rich man, maybe even rich enough to put some covered walkways on campus to keep us dry when it rains. But this isn't something I need to fear with you, Mrs. Jones. We are in it together. We are the 'helpers,' as people like to say. We share a common bond, this silly misconception people have of us, that we are trying to save the world. Of course we know this isn't true. Regardless, the problem with this concept, however, is that when you try and save the world, you end up with very little time and energy to save yourself. Presumably, this is the situation you are confronted with now. I think you and I both know that we aren't trying to fix these kids as if you are working on a car and the transmission went out. We are just trying to give them the tools to fix themselves."

She turned her ear to me, and sat up a little straighter in her chair.

I continued, "To be honest, I don't know anyone else who could take the punishment these students give out, and then turn around and put a smile on their face quite the way you do. You know that in spite of their weaker moments, they absolutely adore you. And truthfully, they may go the rest of their lives never knowing someone

194

who is as supportive of them as you are. Unfortunately, we don't always see the impact others have on us until many years down the road."

Mrs. Jones paused to consider what I had said. She flipped her hair back from her shoulders and looked as if she was ready to put a halt to the somber moment.

Slightly stronger in tone now, she said, "I know. These kids are different." She breathed a big sigh and changed her beat. "They love strong and they hate strong. And I guess if we can be the one constant in their life, we can make a difference even while everything else crumbles around them."

"I agree," I said confidently. "You and I both know it won't happen overnight, but rather one small miracle at a time." I laughed at myself as I acknowledged how cliché I sounded, though hackneyed phrases have their place I suppose.

We paused in silence to absorb the conversation. A silence that was abruptly penetrated, somewhat comedically, as we could hear Duncan cursing in the background, "Damn internet sucks!" "This is bullshit!" We both laughed under our breaths as if we would get in trouble if someone heard us finding amusement in Duncan's inappropriate behavior. *This place is crazy, I* thought to myself, *in the best way possible.*

I extended my hand again, not to offer a tissue this time, but to offer a comforting grip. She looked up at me from beneath her small mountain of tissues and half smiled, a somewhat hopeful smile, "One small miracle at a time," she said, in agreement. "How corny are we?" she said, realizing what she had resigned herself to repeating.

I turned toward the door, not wanting to overextend my welcome and slightly feeling like this conversation had run its course. Mrs. Jones shared my sentiment for the time being, and nodded her head toward the exit of her office. "Thanks for stopping by," she said. "Let's catch up later."

As I turned to leave, I couldn't help but feel heavy with the weight of what we had discussed. I carried it with me momentarily, and it caused me to hang my head and stare at the carpeted floor, which was an outdated, faded pale blue color with small cracks in the seams. *Man they need to do something about these ugly carpets.* As I took my final steps out the office with my head down, I noticed the bouquet of flowers Mrs. Jones had been carrying was now in the trash can, the bright red and yellow petals had been torn and crumbled, the stems broken so they could fit inside the circumference of the trash disposal. *Peculiar.*

"Mr. Clark," she called after me. "Wait, I've been meaning to give you this. So silly of me, I accidentally grabbed the wrong stack of mail that was in your cubby instead of mine." Mrs. Jones lifted several piles of loose papers that could have filled at least two file cabinets. Underneath it all, she pulled a stack of mail with my name on it. "Here you go sweetie."

"Oh, thanks," I said. "More mail to throw away, never anything good ya know? By the way, next time I come back we are organizing this office," I said, sparking a bit of laughter from both of us.

As I took my leave, I shuffled through my mail as I moved through the hallway down to my own work area, curious as to why I even had a cubby for mail in the first place. The only mail I ever got were credit card offers from solicitors; I really had no idea how they found out where I worked. *Evil bastards,* I thought. As I tossed the mail aside on my desk, a loose piece of paper slipped out and fell to the ground. I bent down to pick it up, *Hmm, this looks like a receipt.* Not wanting to give it the time of day, I moved to add it to the stack of my useless mail, but my eyes were drawn to a charge of $34.73. *What did I spend nearly $35 on?* I wondered. As I took another moment to analyze the receipt closer, I realized it wasn't my receipt at all. Across the top it had Mrs. Jones's name written on it. *She must have accidentally gotten her receipt mixed up in my mail. Damn that messy desk of hers.* My heart sank again, as I couldn't help but notice the purchase she had made, $34.73, for one bouquet of flowers, to be delivered to Mrs. Jones at Bishop Secondary School.

Chapter 8

Fish Out of Water

None of us were really sure what he was doing there. It was just after 1:00 pm and the temperature had reached a sweltering 96 degrees, with a heat index of 104 degrees. His brand new blue Mercedes was parked in the visitors spot, otherwise known as the patch of grass outside the main office with "less dirt." Two feet came out of the car door and were firmly planted on the ground. He wore black Kenneth Cole shoes that were freshly polished, matching black dress pants, and a white button down shirt with a goofy tie that looked like cartoon characters were dancing around on it. He took one hand and rubbed his balding head, and then ran his fingers through his meticulously groomed beard as if to make some sort of commanding non-verbal statement. Mr. Campbell liked to look sharp. Clearly, he didn't spend much time at Bishop, otherwise he would have known better than to put forth too much effort towards his outfits. The clothes most of the staff wore who conducted direct therapy services already had faded stains on them from past experiences trying to de-escalate an irate student when food and beverages happened to be around. We never wore anything new to work.

Mr. Campbell stuck out like a sore thumb. He held some high-ranking job with the superintendent's office, but as with most politics, we were never able to figure out exactly what he did or what his specific purpose was. What's worse, I don't think he knew his purpose either. Moreover, staff were a little hazy as to why he would show up unannounced, yet we were obliged to accommodate him nonetheless. We secretly hoped he was working up plans and contemplating methods to improve our campus, perhaps even reallocating funds to enhance our walkways, fix the holes in the portable buildings, repair the fragile, historic wooden steps before someone broke an ankle, and provide some covered walkways for when it rained. Mr. Campbell didn't have experience in education, and he knew frighteningly little about the special education population in particular. Sometimes when he would show up, he might see a student rolling in the grass with his shirt off, a shoeless

Chad running around campus cursing at staff with the vernacular of a foul mouthed comedian on stage, two adults escorting a rabid elementary student to building 15, or maybe one of the kids jumping in the dumpster behind the office and singing songs from a Disney movie. This was all normal for Bishop staff to deal with, but Mr. Campbell always looked utterly bewildered and confused. For that reason, we tried to steer him away from talking to the students, as he surely wouldn't know what to say and more than likely do more harm than good. We also heightened our focus on the students' behaviors when he was around, somewhat worried that one of their outbursts would besmirch the name of our school and scare Mr. Campbell away, cutting off our only hope for a campus facelift.

I approached Mr. Campbell cordially and said, "What brings you to our campus today?"

He puffed out his chest and ran his hands around his belt as if he was bloated from having eaten too much food, which was more than likely the case, "Mr. Cooper, how goes it?" His southern accent was strong, too strong, as if he was forcing it to play some sort of role in how people perceived him.

"Um, it's fine, and it's Clark, not Cooper," I said, slightly annoyed at having corrected him yet again, like I do each visit.

"Of course it is. I meet so many people it's hard to keep up." *If your only job is to meet people you would do well to remember their name. No mind, I was an entry level staff, no one of consequence.* Mr. Campbell liked to do that thing that politicians do, which is to behave as if he was best friends with everyone he spoke with.

Additionally, he made it well known that he was a fan of country buffets. He had no reservations about the time he spent there, regardless of how it affected his weight and overall health. Sweat was soaking through his shirt, as if he had accidentally fallen in a pool. *Did the AC not work in his car?*

He slapped his hand on my back as if we were good ole boys, and said, "I guess I was in the neighborhood and just thought I'd stop by and check on you guys."

I feel your wholehearted concern for me, seeing as how you can't remember my name after all the times you have been here.

"These kids keeping you busy?"

I'm offended by your tie.

"Like you wouldn't believe, I think I got my workout in for the day."

"Ought to get em out here on that basketball court and hit em with some basketball drills to wear em out."

Does he think I'm the P.E. coach?

Though his comment seemed innocuous, it never ceased to amaze me how often an outsider's solution to these students' disturbed behaviors was to exhaust them physically to the point where it was borderline punishment.

It doesn't work that way.

I feigned enthusiasm as if his idea was as fresh as a glass of iced lemon tea on this smoldering hot day. "You know something, you're right, that's a great idea. I'll just..wear em out from now on..."

"Thatta boy!" he said, using his whole body to laugh graciously. He was proud of himself, as if he just gave me an inside tip to the stock market that was going to make me a millionaire. Then came another gratuitous slap on the back, leaving a large sweaty handprint on my shirt.

"So I'm assuming you will want to be speaking to the principal now?" *My effort to get him inside the office before I would need a life jacket to float in the small pond of sweat he was sure to create any second now.*

"No sir, not today. I'm fixin to ingratiate myself amongst the students today. I want to get a feel for what it's like to work with these kids so as I can report back as to what you guys really need out here. Take me to a classroom and let's help somebody."

This is not going to end well.

"Spendid!" I said. *Who can I pawn him off on?* I began to scour through names of staff in my head who could possibly entertain him for a while. Just that second a call came over the walkie-talkie. Mr. Williams spoke over the air loud enough for Mr. Campbell to hear, "Hey Mr. Clark, can you go speak with Katie down in Mrs. Cassidy's room? Something about her computer not working, she has her head down and threatening to run away from class."

"Of course Mr. Williams, and your timing is perfect."

Mr. Campbell looked amused, "Shall we?" I said.

"We shall," he replied.

Here we go…

If one were to take a snapshot of Mrs. Cassidy's classroom, one would see a group of rambunctious middle school students, the class a bustling hive of activity as some students were away from their desks and interacting with one another. It almost looked like an ideal picture of what a classroom is supposed to look like. But there were two misplaced items in the picture. In the corner of the room, Katie sat with her head down on the desk in front of the computer. She was pounding her fists on the desk and kicking her feet against the wall. This was expected. The other piece that would have stood out was a boy named Trey, who sat leaned back in his chair with his legs outstretched, arms folded behind his head, and a troublesome smile across his face. I had seen that look before, more than likely he had something to do with this. Trey enjoyed to presenting a darker image; he dressed in black pants and black shirt every day. He kept his head shaved to reflect the beliefs that he had committed himself to. I was sure I would find out what the menacing smile meant later, and just as sure that I wouldn't want to. Trey began laughing to himself, an ominous laughter.

I'll deal with him later, I thought. *He's not likely to set Mr. Campbell up for success.*

Mrs. Cassidy made her way across the room in her blue Capri pants and red T-shirt that read "live, love, teach" on the front in italicized green writing. She was a confident woman with a no-nonsense attitude, approximately 5'6," who wore her blonde hair in a bun with a pink hair-tie. She took her pink rimmed glasses off to address me and Mr. Campbell.

"Mr. Campbell, what a pleasant surprise." *She's acting,* I thought.

"So what happened?" he said. He held his hands in the air as if he was holding an imaginary ball. "There's a little girl in trouble?" he said, still nurturing the make-believe ball, and looking at us for reassurance.

"Well, something like that. For some reason all my computers just stopped working. There is a dialogue box that we can't click out of, it's like they're frozen. I told all the students to move on to their next reading assignment, but Katie has trouble transitioning, and she was very proud of herself for almost finishing that computer work because she did such a great job. Now she's just sitting with her head down and won't walk away."

A nice time to discuss with Mr. Campbell how our computers are over ten years old and can barely handle a dial up speed connection, I thought. But before I could say anything, Mr. Campbell moved across the room towards Katie, his waist involuntarily moving the students' desks out of his path as if he was a poorly rolled bowling ball slowly knocking through the pins.

He leaned over Katie, who still had her head down. He then rolled his sleeves up as if he was preparing to dig a ditch. Rather than using a neutral, comforting voice, he managed to bellow out the following words, ever so slowly over-accenting his southern tongue, "Well isn't this just a honkey donk?"

What the hell does that mean? I suddenly felt like I was in a cheap, poorly acted western movie.

Katie bent down to tighten her laces, her bright green shorts and pink shirt illustrated her quirky, offbeat personality well. She had a small frame, and chewed on her beaded necklace when she was nervous. She was a sweet girl, but had very low self-esteem. She would often engage in negative self-talk and shut down emotionally. Once she got there, it took 20 to 30 minutes for her to overcome her negative state of mind, supplemented by a great deal of emotional support from staff. This tugged at the emotions of staff who helped her, as Katie was an outwardly charming girl. Her innocent puppy eyes implored you to spoil her.

Katie now turned her head to the side of her folded arms, staring up at this large unknown man standing over her.

"Hey ya little girl, Katelyn right?"

"It's Katie." she snapped stubbornly.

"Course it is. Anyhow, I hear you were doin' some good work, and then up and out of nowhere your computer needs fixin. That about right?" Again Mr. Campbell spoke as if someone had a remote control to his voice-box and had clicked "slow motion."

Katie sat quietly, looking slightly uncomfortable, keen on trying to process the situation rather than answer Mr. Campbell's questions.

"Well you done a good job here, why don't you try and move on to the next assignment? Mrs. Cassidy said so."

"I can't do it!" Katie replied.

"Can't do what?"

"Questions from the book. I'm not good at reading. I'm only good at math," she said innocently.

Mr. Campbell now boasted a look of achievement, a light went off in his head as if he was really getting somewhere.

"Well little darling," he said. "Don't worry too much about it, just do all you can do and let the rough end drag."

That's it Mr. Campbell, use expressions that go right over her head.

Katie sat unmoved, eyebrows furrowed, still not entirely sure what to make of the situation.

"You know what I mean right, just crack the whip!"

Still Katie sat befuddled. Her sad puppy eyes were growing bigger by the second, as if any minute now they would be drooping to the floor and someone would trip over them. After an agonizing minute or two of silence, Mr. Campbell surmised that his progress was somewhat stymied. He looked at me briefly for guidance, apparently surprised he hadn't turned the situation around by now. I rolled my hand in encouraging circles motioning for him to continue, much to my own amusement.

"Well Katie, I think what you need is a fresh outlook, a little can-do attitude. You know you can do this, because can't never could," said Mr. Campbell in impressive fashion, smiling at his own perceived wit. Katie, now approximating what Mr. Campbell was trying to do, clumsily fiddled with the rainbow barrettes in her hair and chewed on her beads. Stubbornly she retorted, "No…I…can't!" "Mr. Fat man!"

Mr. Campbell ran his hands around his waist again and began nervously running his hands through his beard as if these motions were long overdue. He was becoming embarrassed by his lack of progress.

Hesitantly, he pressed on, "Well sure ya can, little darling. And let's stay away from mean words," once again trying to project his make-believe powers onto this sweet little girl. "Ya know, you catch more flies with jam than you do with vinegar." Katie backed her head away, covered her nose, and wafted the air in front of her, insulted by Mr. Campbell's breath.

Another confusing one liner that was sure to save the day, I thought. It was as if he was on a farm, talking casually to the chickens as he dropped the bird feed to the ground, never expecting an actual response. Katie was now growing increasingly perturbed by Mr. Campbell's presence, as well as his perplexing choice of words, and she showed her frustration. 'I can't do it! I can't do it! I can't do it!" replied Katie, now tucking her head back in her arms. "I'm stupid," her voice echoed from the cave she created between her arms wrapped around her head and the desk.

Mr. Campbell's face turned slightly red, and drops of sweat gathered beneath him. Desperate for air, he was beginning to lose patience. He had preordained that he was simply going to walk in the classroom and snap his fingers and see the situation resolved. Another microcosm of a much larger picture. Most people don't understand these students. That's why they are here, that's why you leave it to professionals who specialize in this sort of thing. That's why powers to be withhold funding from schools like this, so they can keep their suits and ties on, take long lunch breaks, and talk about their next golfing tournament.

Mr. Campbell made one last ditch effort to save the day, "You *CAN* do it, you *ARE* a smart girl, and…and you CAN do it!" he said with contempt and frustration.

Katie now pulled her head out of her folded arms and sat up straight, "Don't say that to me! I told you *I CAN'T* do it and I'm stupid." Mr. Campbell would now violate one of the basic rules at Bishop, never argue with a student. You will always lose. He was to now belittle himself by stooping to Katie's level, engaging in an unwinnable argument with an unmannerly little girl who was just getting warmed up.

"Well I said you're *NOT* stupid and you *CAN!*"

"I AM stupid and *I CAN'T!"*

"CAN!"

"CAN'T"

"CAN!"

"CAN'T!"

"CAN!"

"CAN'T!"

"CAN!"

"CAN'T!"

"Alright fine!" bellowed Mr. Campbell and his voice rumbled through the classroom as if there was an earthquake. Katie now looked somewhat satisfied, as if her spirits had been ever so slightly lifted at having gotten a rise out of this cheeky fella. Her sassy behavior had been rewarded by Mr. Campbell's newfound acquiescence to defeat. Sweating and visibly agitated, he callously peered down at Katie, deciding he would have the last word, and said, "You know what, I changed my mind. You CAN'T do it! You're stupid! You're never gonna go anywhere and never gonna be anything. Is that what you want to hear? Ha!"

Bravo.

The room froze. Mrs. Cassidy and I both froze. The students, even the ones who were previously nonchalant towards the situation, all held their breath to see what would happen next. It is the split second in time, when the tightrope walker suddenly loses his balance. He knows it, the crowd knows it, and the only scientific explanation for what will happen next is the sheer 200 foot drop to his death. Or more simply put, cause and effect.

Katie, sweet Katie, straightened her back and the sad puppy eyes that were almost filling up the room rapidly changed into a look of ferocity. She clenched her jaw tight and cocked her head to the side in disbelief. I shared a look with Mrs. Cassidy to assure her that we were both equally mortified.

Katie was preparing to raise hell. Her ferocious eyes met Mr. Campbell's with unrestricted savage intent, "YOU CAN'T FUCKING TALK TO ME THAT WAY! GO TO FUCKING HELL FUCKER!" Katie screamed an ear-splitting shriek and shot up from her seat as if Mr. Campbell had raised the dead, her head still cocked, and body poised to spring into action. Mr. Campbell was downright stupefied, as if he was a magician fooled by his own trick. He backpedaled into the desk behind him. "Hey man watch your ass!" a student cried. He didn't acknowledge the voice behind him, "That's not supposed to happen!" he said, scared of the monster he had awakened in Katie.

Katie leapt from her desk and smashed the computer to the floor in one swift motion. I moved to grab her but wasn't able to circumvent Mr. Campbell's rotund body. He maintained a look of horror and humiliation as he moved to set his back against the wall. Katie leapt onto a nearby desk. On her tip toes, she danced her way across the room using the other students' desks as her platform to keep her from ever touching the ground. Her strides were long yet light, as if she was a pole vaulter gaining confidence before launching herself into the air and clearing the horizontal bar. She had improvised one hell of an obstacle course while the other students watched and cheered her on. "Katie! Katie! Katie!" they chanted in encouragement. Katie's feet hit the ground with grace as she aimed to make her grand exit. On her way out of the room, she grabbed and flipped over a bookshelf that tumbled to the ground, receiving more rapturous applause from her peers, who looked at her with reverence. Her momentum enabled her to burst through the classroom door so hard that it slammed against the outside railing with a thunderous impact, before disappearing. All eyes looked towards the exit, as the only action left to the demolishment of the room was to hear the door close, affirming the chaos that had come to pass. However, just before the door shut completely, a small hand reappeared in the crack between the wall and the door, flaunting purple sparkly nail polish. Katie reemerged as she swung the door back open with conviction. A mischievous smile swept across her face and she flicked the light switch from the on to off position just for good measure. Looking at Mr. Campbell, she raised her middle finger, "You're a stupid man," she said, just before taking a bow, and left us all in the dark classroom.

Mr. Campbell and I moved to charge outside the classroom, but we both tried to exit at the same time and wound up getting sandwiched in the threshold of the doorway, completely immobile. *Somebody get this guy out of here.* Aggravated, I shouted, "Back up, I'll go first!" and broke free as he stepped back. After the conundrum, we scanned the campus to locate Katie. She was ten feet off the ground in a nearby tree, where she made herself quite comfortable, already forming a pillow out of a bed of leaves.

I looked at Mr. Campbell as if to say *Thanks a lot.* In truth, Katie had climbed trees before, and it was nothing I couldn't handle, as long as Mr. Campbell stayed as far away as possible.

"Want me to try to talk her down?" he said, bashfully.

"I think I'll take it from here."

"Guess I'm a fish outta water round these parts," he said reluctantly.

This is Bishop, I thought to myself.

Chapter 9

Black Hat

I felt like a firefighter pulling a cat from a tree. Down came Katie with a smile on her face, relieved from her clash with heights. I felt a tap on my shoulder and turned around, "Trevor, why are you out of class again?" I said, slightly annoyed. I tried to shift my mindset seamlessly from Katie to Trevor, not sure who was more deserving of my attention at the moment.

"Look at my new friend." He motioned towards his forearm and raised it just parallel to his head, where a white caterpillar freckled with orange and black spots rested motionless.

I felt discombobulated from Mr. Campbell's interference; Trevor's needs ranked low on my priority list for the moment. I decided to take a shortcut to get Trevor to class. I looked closer at the caterpillar, studying its features. With a nervous face and impatient tone, I told him, "That caterpillar is poisonous. He could bite you and your arm could fall off. I'd leave him alone if I were you!"

Trevor's eyes grew big, he shrieked, and fear overtook his face. With a flick of his arm the caterpillar was sent flying through the air, only to land on the laces of Trevor's astronaut shoes. He picked up a nearby stick and nudged the caterpillar off his shoe. Katie laughed as Trevor danced around trying to free himself of the venomous caterpillar, which was no closer to posing a threat than Trevor himself.

"You're lucky I saved you," I said, as if waiting for a thank you. "I may not be here next time to warn you, which is another good reason why you should go to class. I gripped my walkie-talkie, placing a call out over the air loud enough for Trevor to hear, "Letting all staff know that if Trevor leaves class again, he is going to drop a level on his behavior chart, which means no fun for him next time we throw a party for the students who don't have problems being where they're supposed to be."

"Man that is bogus! This place is horsecrap!" cried Trevor, never allowing himself to actually say a curse word.

"Don't push it Trevor, just go where you're supposed to be."

I thought it strange I hadn't heard any response over the air.

"I know why the computers don't work in Mrs. Cassidy's class," said Trevor casually, still overstaying his welcome.

"Oh really, and why is that?"

"What will you give me if I tell you?"

"What exactly do y___, 'Attention staff, your communication systems have been taken over. Your technology is now under my control, please send a negotiator to building 11.'"

Mrs. Cassidy's room. Building 11 was exactly where I had just come from. And that voice was not the voice of a staff member. As much as I hated to admit it, I knew there was something more sinister at play with those computers, even if they *were* outdated pieces of junk.

"Trevor, go to class," I insisted, foreshadowing chaos. "And make sure you get to the bus on time today please, you can't keep holding up the rest of the kids for your nature hunts." Trevor turned to walk away before uttering a bratty "Aw man!" as his voice trailed away from me.

Katie was under control now to where I trusted she could find her way to Mr. Morales's office. I looked at my watch, 2:00pm on the nose, *roughly one more hour to go before I could call it a day.* A lot can happen at Bishop in an hour.

Mrs. Cassidy's class sat outside the building in the grass, as instructed to do when the classroom was inoperable. Grant interrupted my path to make sure I knew one of his important facts that simply couldn't wait until later. "Jimmy Page dated a 14 year old girl while he was touring with Led Zeppelin, are you still planning on playing guitar with me later today?" he said in one swift run-on sentence, completely unaware that those two ideas are disconnected and form two very different thoughts.

"That really all depends on how the next 15 minutes go in here," I said. "I can't guarantee it, but I will try my hardest to be there."

"Gotta be there bro, let's jam!" replied Grant. "Like I said, I'll do my best." I responded again, with no degree of certainty.

Some students playfully pushed and shoved; some secretly operated their cell phones as discretely as possible; some tossed a football in the air; and Mrs. Cassidy sat casually on the grass, shuffling through a stack of papers in her lap as she made notes with her red pen. Everything about the situation was routine. Other than the oppressive August heat, the students showed no reluctance regarding their current delay. I approached the rickety brown steps again cautiously, holding tight to the railing, never knowing if my foot would be enough weight to break the old steps once and for all.

"Good luck," muttered Mrs. Cassidy sardonically, knowing that I would surely be walking into a tense and awkward situation. I twisted the silver door knob to building 11. There were several small dents on the door knob revealing its history of having been bashed with inanimate objects, forcing me to toggle the knob several times to gain access. Once inside, I stepped over the fallen bookshelf, with the spines of several books open and facing the ceiling. I silently credited Katie for her efficient handiwork. The lights were still off; the switch on the opposite wall, across a pool of more debris. In the center of the room sat Trey, who was staring out the window until I entered. In his hand he held a black walkie talkie he had used to air his message; across the bottom was a white label with black font that read "Mr. Smith." *So Mr. Smith's walkie-talkie works after all.*

Trey lifted his feet onto the desk in front of him, exposing his tightly laced combat boots, which were a hand-me-down from his dad. He crossed one leg over the other before placing his hands behind his head as if he was considering an afternoon nap. He was a blur of black pants and a long black shirt.

Trey had a tempestuous relationship with the school's technology support, given his lengthy history of tampering with computers, breaking the school's firewall, and logging on to websites that were restricted. Trey developed these hobbies out of a necessity to earn the negative attention he craved. Even for Bishop, Trey was a different, anxious, and solitary teenager. He was extremely proud of his perfect attendance record.

Although his time outside of school was spent in isolation, racking up hundreds and thousands of hours of unsupervised computer activity. It was here he developed internet followers who would later applaud his community ruses he recorded. Every month or so, a video would surface on the internet where he would confront a police officer, baiting the man with a badge into a conversation about Trey's constitutional rights. With the intent of provocation, he would carry a camera in his hand, practically begging the officer to make a mistake. This way Trey could post the video online and achieve overnight fame. Above all else, Trey craved the spotlight.

He didn't have very many friends, his preference instead to make people uneasy reinforced him much more acutely than what a typical friendship could offer. In friendly, quiet neighborhoods he could be seen lurking along the side roads or walking through private yards, inviting watchful residents to send a patrol unit to their aid, which almost certainly came to pass with each effort. He operated with a kind of excessive, single-minded zeal. The star of his own videos, he would record his entire conversation with the patrol officer, as if Trey himself was inconvenienced by the police officer's response to worried homeowners. But it was all a game to him, "How dare you abridge my freedom of speech, you're infringing on my rights," he would say. "What's the matter? A guy can't just simply walk through the neighborhood with a video camera and a long black coat and combat boots in the middle of July?" he could be found saying, as he proclaimed his innocence.

Trey gave local law enforcement officers such a headache that the online blogs he authored and the videos he was responsible for were subsequently used in training scenarios for new officers, so that they knew what to do with his defiant, argumentative personality type, one who was a self-professed expert on constitutional rights. Trey harbored some of the characteristics of other Bishop students: impulsivity, anger, resentment, and aggression. What made him different was a lack of impulsivity. He took calculated, methodical risks, to which there was always more than meets the eye. For this reason, Trey was difficult to trust. I spent extra time running my metal detector around him each morning for good measure. At some point I got used to seeing the students' files long list of running diagnoses. As for Trey, "behaviors congruent with disruptive mood dysregulation disorder, paranoid schizophrenia, and obsessive compulsive disorder" all blended together creating a perfect storm. The explanation of Trey's disorders and how they manifested was never difficult to grasp, but the root cause always proved unobtainable. If not handled carefully, he could easily place himself or someone else at risk of harm.

Obsessed with German history and Nazism, Trey felt this interest boosted his efforts to be a self-made "black hat." My knowledge on this nickname was loosely based on some information I read in passing while looking into Trey's background. From what I gathered, there exist essentially two main behavior classes of hackers. The "white hats" sought out flaws in technology systems in hopes of exposing loopholes that would eventually lead to new safeguards that benefit the public. Alternatively, the "black hats" were made up of people with obsessive compulsive personality types with their own malicious agendas. Much like Trey, the black hats wanted to be simultaneously feared and worshipped. While Trey's behaviors hadn't yet escalated to the point where he threatened anyone's public safety, he was well on his way. A part of me had to acknowledge that Trey's fixation with technology enabled him to carve a path that would one day lead to him conducting large-scale technological sabotage. There was little to stop him from walking into a public library and sabotaging innocent people's personal information, maxing out credit cards that didn't belong to him, stealing identities, or transferring money into his account from a remote location.

Trey shifted his weight menacingly, casually drawing on his desk with a number 2 pencil. As he scratched his chin I couldn't help but notice dirt under his fingernails. I studied what he was drawing for a few seconds, it was some sort of odd shaped cross. Mrs. Cassidy must have removed the students from the room once she became aware Trey confiscated the walkie talkie. If history is any indication, it was about to get akward. He glared at me and pushed his glasses up so they sat properly on his pointed nose. He had the room to himself until I walked in, he was king. I was trespassing in his newfound territory. I stared at him inquisitively, waiting to see who would talk first. Then he spoke in a proud voice that indicated he was amused with himself, "I see you got my message."

I ditched the formalities, "Yea, I heard you on the walkie talkie, as I was climbing down from a tree, oddly enough. Aren't you hot in those boots?"

"You never know when you need to form a militia," Trey said.

Choosing to ignore that comment, I asked, "Is there something that you want? Mrs. Cassidy needs to get her class back inside. Come up to the office where it's more comfortable and have a chat? Mr. Morales is up there too."

Trey scoffed at me, glanced over at the two computers at the computer station, one still on the floor. I got the hint he was annoyed that I hadn't acknowledged his work locking his classmates out of the computers.

"I hope Katie recovers. That meltdown may cost her a field trip or two. It's nice knowing I can trigger people like that, all with the press of a few buttons." Here was proof now that Trey was the reason the computer stopped working, which subsequently lead to Katie's ill-timed tirade. Trey waited, stared at me intently, salivating at the thought of me putting the facts together, desperately awaiting my reaction. Trey wanted to be authenticated. Had this been an interrogation perhaps I would have played his game and massaged his ego. But I stayed silent and unimpressed, not wanting to oblige him.

Trey puffed his chest out, staring at me menacingly. I noted his palpable desire to manipulate the conversation. He waited for me to express my disappointment, say something about the poor choice he made and how horribly it affected Katie, such that she was devastated and might never recover. But only a fool would fall into his trap. If I were to play his games, I would prolong the resolution of the situation, Trey would stay right where he was, and the class of students could not return. The important task at hand was not about boosting Trey's confidence and forming a fragile alliance to cajole him out of the room, as this would only take up precious time and energy. Preventing a class from learning was wholly unacceptable, encroaching on student rights that are taken with utmost seriousness. I had been in similar situations before, and the only agenda I was concerned with at this point was giving Trey a fair chance to make a responsible decision to simply leave the classroom. The rest of the pieces could be dealt with afterwards. The best option was one that would hopefully carry Trey outwards and onwards from the room. I would move to incapacitate his ego.

"Katie's great, actually. She apologized for her behavior, says she learned a lot from the situation. I'm really proud of her. She is on her way to class, and the computers, they should be fixed in no time."

Trey's insatiable thirst for control was powerful, and I had just rendered him parched. He began seething. His eyes darted down to his drawing and he fixed has jawline rigid, as if I had insulted his entire existence. He wasn't expecting this. His free hand gripped the edge of the desk, either preparing for an earthquake, or preparing to rip the top off the desk. He was clearly uncomfortable, immensely agitated at my unexpected response. As his body betrayed him, I noticed a drop of sweat from his eyebrow; he tried to appear casual as he set his pencil down and wiped it away with his pointer finger. He breathed impatiently as if something significant was on his mind. He started to speak, but his overwhelming sense of dissatisfaction with this outcome paralyzed his mouth so that he wasn't able to form the words. Trey, ordinarily fluid and verbose, began stuttering and stammering in a barely sustainable, childish, staccato like rage, "F...Fu...Fuck that!" I had only heard it once before, but Trey stuttered when he was uncomfortable. I began to feel slightly apologetic towards him for the physiological reaction I caused.

"Trey," I said again, calmly, but slightly more assertive and impatient now, "What are we doing here?"

"You tell me..." he said. Lost and confused, desperate for an escape plan to save face, Trey leaned on his most comfortable subject material, the argument that earned him online followers of his blogs. "You tell me why black people can call each other niggers but white people say that word and then black people get pissed?" he snapped, as he cocked his head sideways. It was a petulant attempt to regain some control of the situation in which he felt helpless. Trey longed to regain stability, trying to rekindle something, anything, that would

232

instigate a semblance of a political or racial litigation that he could feel good about. This was his agenda.

Sensing I had to give a little to get a little, I gave him an inch or so by answering his question. "There is a long history of white people using that word derogatively towards the black race, a history I'm sure you are aware of," I said.

Trey thought briefly I would appeal to his emotional stances concerning his racial and discriminative sensitivities. He began to spout out a number of rehearsed and programmed responses, "Affirmative action takes jobs away from white people!" I quickly washed away his renewed sense of purpose.

"This is a conversation that is better suited for a private office. The racial discussion isn't going any further, besides that is something you can talk about with your counselor," I said, not remotely willing to indulge him.

"So you are going to violate my right to free speech?" he replied. "Did you know that since the year 2000 about 1,000,000 immigrants come to this country and steal our fucking jobs, steal my dad's job?"

"Trey, you are holding up a class from learning. I know we have talked before about how when you feel this way, you ask your teacher if you can come up to the office and talk with me or Mr. Morales. It's really that simple. This isn't the right way to express yourself." I still wanted to be careful not to acknowledge the fact that he had indeed created a tremendous inconvenience for his class, for me, for Katie, as well as the computers, which surely would take hours to recover. To belabor this point in the moment was to empower him.

"There you go again, violating my rights." Still desperate, Trey wanted to continue moving his chess pieces around the board, but I wouldn't offer him opposition in his effort to methodically lay a trap, so that he could take up the rest of the day arguing with me. Again, I threw a wet rag on his ploy with some impromptu jargon of my own.

"Your rights aren't being violated. On this campus you are still bound by the rules of the school. Right now, you are disrupting campus because you won't leave the classroom and you are preventing other students from the education rights *they* are entitled to," I said, with a hint of urgency. "As far as your rights go, the conversation ends there. If you want people to follow rules then you should start following them yourself. I'd appreciate it if you would calmly walk up to the office."

Trey now seemed beside himself with disappointment. But instead of acting on his anger, he began laughing forcibly. I didn't want to know why he was laughing or what he was cooking up in his head, yet an eerie feeling swept over me. Frustrated at all of his attempts to assert his perceived superiority, Trey continued his dry laugh. He picked his head up from his desk, and began methodically licking his lips, his tongue out as if he was tasting a dish. He leaned his head back authoritatively and looked down on me as if he was higher ranking, his voice robotic now, "Don't you want to know what I'm laughing at?"

"I want you to be okay, Trey." I said, genuinely concerned, but offering no further response, as I would inevitably hear Trey answer his own question. Without further hesitation, Trey's silver buckles on his shoes collided with the legs of his chair and made a clanking noise. Trey climbed up onto the seat of his desk and was now standing 10 feet tall. "Is anyone really okay?" he asked, appearing to no one in particular. Amused with himself, he started marching in a stationary position on his desk, bringing his right knee up to his chest and back down again, then his left, stomping on the seat of his desk as if he would break it. Shortly thereafter, he began singing:

"Es braust unser Panzer im Sturmwind dahin"

"Es braust unser Panzer im Sturmwind dahin"

"It's called Panzerlized, Mr. Clark! You know it! It's a German war song."

My head was spinning. *This is escalating quickly,* I thought.

"Es braust unser Panzer im Sturmwind dahin"

"Es braust unser Panzer im Sturmwind dahin"

Trey continued to march in place reciting imperfect German.

"Mr. Williams," I called boldly over the air, as if I was daring anyone else with a walkie-talkie to try and interrupt my message.

"Go ahead, Clark. What's the update on Trey?"

"Well, listen to the background noise," I said, as I held down the receiver to the walkie-talkie while Trey screamed over me,

"Es braust unser Panzer im Sturmwind dahin"

"Es braust unser Panzer im Sturmwind dahin"

"Mr. Clark, I don't know what the heck that noise is," he responded.

"Yea, that's why I'm calling, I may need assistance down here with Trey, he's not leaving class, just putting on a show." I could feel my skin crawling, I held resolute.

"Ok Clarky, I'll be ready to put the word out should you need it. Just let me know." he replied.

"Clarky," was the informal name I was given when staff wanted to lighten me up. My face was marked with exhaustion, my patience running thin. But there was no way Mr. Williams could have seen that from his desk. He must have felt a smidge of what I was going through by the urgency in my voice. Little did I know, the situation was about to turn decidedly dark. Had I known, I would have requested additional staff in an instant.

Trey replaced marching and singing with laughing again. I paused, hoping he would move on. "Mr. Clark, you haven't asked me why I'm still laughing! I'll just go ahead and tell you. I'm laughing because these computers don't work, because you know what? I ran a waterhole attack, basically did it with my eyes closed." I would later come across literature that described a waterhole attack as a subtle method of hacking where the hacker takes advantage of a popular network that many people share, such as a coffee shop, bar, or *school.* The hacker creates some sort of fake wireless access point and takes advantage of people's personal information. In this case, Trey hadn't run a true waterhole attack; fortunately, he wasn't that skilled yet. He only thought he was. His diabolical motivation was still in place, but thankfully the outcome was less damaging. Trey had somehow accessed the computers as an administrator, and downloaded malicious files that were harmful to the computer, rendering them useless. After all of this, he *still* hadn't let go of wanting me to feel impressed. If I showed shock, or disappointment, he would feel happy with himself. He continued on boasting and bragging about his abilities.

I spoke into the walkie-talkie again, Trey was getting under my skin. I was trying sincerely not to show a single smidge of agitation, or Trey would win. As neutrally and indifferently as I could possibly feign, I called out, "Okay Mr. Williams, I'm requesting administrative privileges to suspend Trey for the day if he doesn't walk out of the classroom right now, can you run that by our principal?"

"Stand by, Clarky."

Trey ceased all activity. I knew from past experiences with Trey that suspension meant a great deal to him. Due to his obsessive compulsive fixations, he always showed consternation over his academics, and upheld his perfectly intact attendance record. It seems I would play the chess game after all. I hoped the threat of suspension would be enough to influence Trey to leave the room so as not to tarnish his perfect attendance record. Trey stared at me again, furious over the card I was playing. The moment was tense like the draw on a bow and arrow. Trey had paused, I had paused, and there was complete radio silence. Mr. Williams's voice sliced through the air from my walkie-talkie, "That's a green light for suspension if he doesn't leave the classroom right away."

"You hear that, Trey? You don't walk out of class now you are suspended. Walk up to the office with me, and let's put this behind us."

Pulsing, Trey looked down towards the ground with a scrunched up nose, as if he had lost his thought and the answer was lying somewhere on the floor. His eyes moved from the floor and back to me; he looked me up and down, as if he was imagining me in a different image, though I didn't know what. Trey jumped down from atop the desk and squared up with me. He didn't yell, scream, or make exaggerated movements, like I half expected. He just looked at me quizzically, then a nerve-racking, coldhearted voice came out of him. I could smell his breath, which reeked of stale onions. The school lunch had done him no favors. His voice trembled and came out just above a whisper, saying, "I was actually laughing earlier because I just had the thought of shooting you in the face..."

I froze. I heard things like this several times a day from a variety of students, and my heart never skipped a beat. But most of these threats from students were empty, something said in the midst of a tirade that didn't carry over with any meaning. But Trey was different. He was a teenager approaching adulthood, and despite his petulant cries and arguments, such threats were credible, given that he had means and potential intent to accomplish this goal. The relationship between the school and Trey's parents wasn't strong, which made communication weak. That he had several arrests for carrying weapons in public didn't ease my mind. We didn't know what gangs Trey had been exposed to, or what guns and weapons he could access. By taking Trey at his word meant that such a threat carried weight.

I can't ignore that one.

My response, "Deputy Richards to building 11 immediately."

"Don't know what to tell you, Clarky, Deputy Richards isn't here. He hasn't gotten back yet from taking Kenny to the hospital."

"Whose side are you on? Are you with me or the niggers and immigrants stealing our jobs and raping this country?" bellowed Trey, as he stared at me with an empty eyes; he was physically present, but simply not there.

I questioned how well I scanned Trey with the metal detector earlier that morning. In my mind, I replayed the process of moving the detector up and down his body, around his shoes, his waistline, the back of his shirt, and his coat pockets. *How well did I listen for beeps? Was I in a hurry? Was I distracted?* While replaying this image from the morning, my heart raced and a darkness washed over me as I realized Trey showed up late to school. I didn't scan him, which meant he could be carrying a gun.

Trey must have heard the deputy wasn't around because
he felt a surge of confidence and leapt forward.
Overweight for his age, he began marching in my
direction and upturning the remaining desks that were in
his way. I backpedaled and turned to take my leave,
never taking my eyes off Trey, who was rifling through his
own pockets in search of something. The rules were
clear--don't entangle oneself physically with a student if it
isn't necessary. There were no students in the room, no
reason for me to stick around alone, the risk was too
great. *But what if Trey did have a gun? I couldn't let him
leave the classroom and endanger the lives of other
students.* As the voice inside me ferociously ricocheted
off opposite parts of my brain, my movement was
restricted by the fallen bookshelf blocking the closed
door. I could hear the students' voices on the other side. I
motioned for my walkie-talkie again to follow up with
another call for backup, but Trey was too close for
comfort now. I could smell his hot breath again. Trey
threw his weight into me and forced my back against the
wall and we stumbled into the shelves behind us, the
books bouncing off my feet. Before I could place a call for

help, my attention was turned to Trey's hand as he continued his motion to pull something out of his pocket. The rules about placing your hands on students were unambiguous. The student had to be placing himself or someone else in immediate harm. After a brief second's consideration, I decided this more than qualified. I quickly seized Trey's arm, not wanting whatever he was retrieving to have a fair chance at being secured in his hand.

"Take your hand out of your pocket!" I demanded.

Trey tensed, he was breathing heavily and had a fearsome look of determination. Trey and I locked eyes. His rotund figure gave him a low center of gravity. "Clarky, everything okay? Do you need extra staff to remove Trey?" I heard Mr. Williams's voice over my earpiece. Trey wasn't athletic, and he wasn't sure what maneuver he was doing or how he wanted this to end. In his haste he stomped on my feet with his combat boots and his free hand moved to grasp the front of my shirt, accidentally grabbing the wire to my walkie-talkie. Realizing this accomplishment, he ripped the connecting cord from my ear and threw it on the ground, preventing me from responding to Mr. Williams. I continued to hold my ground, burdened with the responsibility of keeping Trey physically safe and bringing as little harm to him as possible while also de-escalating the situation. I wasn't able to call for backup from any other staff. I was alone. *Surely Mr. Williams would send more staff, but how long would that take?* I was plagued with the thought of accidentally hurting Trey, *What if nothing threatening was in his pocket, I'll have overreacted, and possibly lose my job, the school could get sued, who knows?* I thought. The struggle continued over the unknown object in his pocket and my grip on his wrist grew tighter, I flexed my entire arm to outmatch his adrenaline fueled rage.

"I'm gonna fuck you up!" Trey screamed.

Trey and I exchanged a grave look.

"Stop, Trey. You need to stop." Trey didn't stop.

I remained as calm as possible. "Stop, Trey," I said again. I scoured my options. *I could wait this out until someone comes, but who knows what will happen in the meantime? I could somehow pin Trey down to the ground, but I still don't know what is in his pocket, a gun*

*could accidentally go off upon impact with a hard surface.
Or I could think of something to say that would stop Trey
long enough for me to tie up his hands and restrain him. I
was starting to lose my temper. I could feel myself
unwinding, bowing to the stress of the situation, not sure
of what I would do if Trey continued.* My adrenaline was
surging, ready to fire on all cylinders in an instant. With
each second that passed, I came closer to the decision
that Trey needed to end up against the wall with his arms
pinned behind his back, and I was going to stop being so
nice. I had almost committed to this decision, but I threw
out one last effort to distract him.

"Now is a good time to remind you that everything you
are doing is on the classroom security cameras."

This reminder caught Trey by surprise, long enough for
the second door to the classroom to swing open. Mr.
Morales and Deputy Richards cleared their way across
the room. Mr. Morales saw how centered my attention
was on Trey's arm that I restrained; he leapt over the
felled desks and doubly secured this arm further by
controlling Trey's elbow with both hands. Deputy
Richards took control of Trey, using this perfectly

justifiable opportunity to assert his dominance, bending him swiftly face first over the only remaining desk and reaching for the handcuffs attached to his belt. Trey had three adults restraining him, he grunted and retched in discomfort, as his face was sandwiched onto the surface of the desk. Surprisingly, Trey acquiesced to defeat and cooperatively, placed his arms behind his back while the handcuffs were placed around his wrists.

Something strange happened, a twinkle formed in his eye. He seemed better already. It was as if the cold steel on his wrists relieved him of some mental ailment. *Is this what he wanted?* I couldn't help but ask myself. The three of us stood nearby, and with Trey's body hunched forward, the Deputy searched Trey's pockets. *Was it a gun?* I thought. We waited with bated breath, unsure of what the outcome would be. There was a jingle of Deputy Richards's keys as he pulled a pair of brass knuckles out of Trey's pocket that had my name on it. "Deputy, I thought you were gone?" Trey quipped. Before muscling Trey out of the classroom, Deputy Richards turned towards me, "looks like I got back just in time," he said sarcastically.

On the way out of the room, Trey looked at me playfully, "I was just kidding Mr. Clark. Why do you have to take things so seriously? Don't you know I want to be a comedian?"

Mr. Morales looked at me now, both of us slightly out of breath, "You okay there gringo?"

I chuckled a depressing laugh.

"I was passing by our security camera monitors in the office, and happened to see you wrestling with him. I caught the Dep on the way out of the office as he pulled in the parking lot. I pointed towards the building and he jumped out of his car and we ran in here, almost called a code red."

"Yea, thought it was a gun." I responded.

"Figured. I don't think Trey would bring a gun to school. Still, better to grab him and find out it wasn't a gun than to wait around and see that it was." he said.

"Yea, brass knuckles can still leave a mark." He nodded in agreement, neither of us being dramatic about the possible outcome that may have come to pass. "I wonder what it means, all this."

"You wonder what?"

"The point of all that. What was he trying to do? Trying to prove?"

"Only Trey knows the answer to that. He has some master plan no doubt."

"Yea, well, I wonder where brass knuckles and being arrested comes into play."

"You think he would've used them on you?" asked Mr. Morales.

"I don't really know. Look in his eyes said yes. Didn't want to line up and give him a free shot though. I take enough hits on the rugby field, though new scars might improve my intimidation factor." I said, trying to uplift the moment.

"You remember that time Trey was spouting out his racist comments and he called me an Islamic terrorist?" Mr. Morales said. I blurted out laughing. "Absolutely. You kept telling him you're Cuban, but he wouldn't listen."

He returned the laughter and shifted his weight from side to side. He pulled his keys out, still attached to the yellow, nylon string, and spun them in circles as he talked.

"Well that's the point. Sometimes you can't make sense of the student's decisions. Don't sweat it. You did everything right. We have our weekly team meeting today. I'll bring this up and we will talk about the situation productively with the teachers and behavior team. You shouldn't have been in here that long without someone else here. More importantly, I'll find out who checked Trey in today when he got to school. Whoever it was apparently forgot to scan him for weapons. Maybe it was one of the new employees. We know how Trey is, we have to learn from it, have to do better."

"He going to lock up tonight?" I asked.

"Trey will have to be arrested, yes. Bishop is flexible but it's not that flexible. Can't come at people with brass knuckles. This one has to go in the books. You agree?" he asked pensively.

"Yea, its just...I don't know. Seems like he wanted that outcome, for some reason."

Mr. Morales stood contemplatively. "Maybe you are right. Time will tell. When you are ready, come up and fill out a report. You know the drill. I guess I owe you some chicken wings, now, right?"

"I'll be taking you up on that. I just need a minute." Acknowledging this, Mr. Morales went outside to speak to Mrs. Cassidy's class. As the door swung closed behind him, he could be heard addressing the students, "Who wants some bonus points for cleaning up the class?" The students, who had no knowledge of what actually happened in the room, chalked it up to another kid acting up, and cheered at the thought of extra points to earn them their favorite activity or community outing.

The classroom was in shambles. Before the students returned, I stood quietly, reflecting on the moments that had just passed, searching for some sort of meaning. Around my feet lay upturned desks, pens, calculators, student backpacks, and a messy array of papers. One paper in particular stood out, and I gently bent over to collect it. I vaguely recognized it as the piece of paper Trey was drawing on, turning it over to have a closer look. My eyes adjusted as my curiosity peaked. I realized I was familiar with this picture he had been drawing. I recognized it to be the picture of a swastika symbol. I stared intently at the design as if it was going to give me an answer to the questions running through my head. *What was the point of all that? How did Trey escalate so quickly? What if another moment or two had gone by, what would I have done?*

I was met with nothing but deafening silence until all my questions narrowed into one. *Maybe Mrs. Jones was right. What are we doing here?*

.

Chapter 10

Comfortably Numb

"It's an F chord, and then a C chord, right?" said Grant, as he moved his fingers across the frets along the neck of the guitar.

"Well yea, but your fingers are wrong. You said C chord but you're forming a D chord instead."

"Oh, that makes sense. Man I'm a goof! I can't hardly keep up with all these chords. I feel like I have to have alien fingers to reach the frets on the guitar."

He was in need of a haircut, his brown mop head was looking like it needed washing, complimented by his black Ramones T-shirt and camouflage pants. He squinted his beady brown eyes when he spoke, and when he laughed he exposed his dimples. Grant was in the minority at Bishop. No one had ever seen him lose his temper or so much as give a rude look to anyone. He was as cool as a cucumber.

"You don't have to have alien fingers," I said. "You just have to spend a lot of time building up the dexterity in your fingers, teaching them to be more flexible and nimble. Before too long they will remember the patterns and you won't have to think too hard about what you are doing. And we can focus on you singing and letting us hear that beautiful voice of yours…"

"Said no one ever!" replied Grant in the midst of laughing. "I can't sing worth a fart!"

"What does that even mean?" I asked. "Nevermind, I don't want to know."

One of the paraprofessionals volunteered to teach guitar lessons from time to time. It wasn't something he had to do, rather an opportunity to expose the students to something they might otherwise never come in contact with. The majority of students had yet to acquire the patience it takes to play an instrument. Therefore, when I had the opportunity, I would swing by his lessons to help him field a few questions from the students as they bombarded him with requests. Not that I was much good; I barely knew more than a few chords myself, but I could play what I knew consistently. The school couldn't afford new guitars on its modest budget; students had to bring in their own somehow, or use several of the donated guitars that were one step short of being completely useless. From where I was sitting across from Grant, I could smell the rotting wood of his guitar that had gotten saturated at some point and emanated a moldy stench. The sounds of poorly tuned guitars and the slapping of wrong notes resonated within the room as they were played by other students. As a self-taught musician, a recreational drummer and saxophonist, it was hard to listen to. Nevertheless, each time one of the kids held a guitar and stroked its strings, their reaction of pure joy made it feel like it was their first time all over again. Although my ears were offended, I was relieved at two thoughts. The first being how awful I must have sounded the first time I began playing an instrument, invoking the need for me to build my tolerance. The second and more important, was how perfectly happy the students were just for the opportunity to create noise. Noting this, a warm feeling washed over me.

I had never seen Grant take such good care of anything; his cd player, his school folders, everything he owned was worn down from Grant's likeliness of being clumsy and rough. To the contrary, he handled the guitar delicately like a precious jewel. After each lesson he did something none of the other students ever did. He would take a red handkerchief he brought from home, and begin methodically wiping the guitar free of handprints and dust. He manipulated the neck of the guitar as if it might break if he squeezed too hard, pressing its body close against his stomach for comfort. Grant knew just about everything one could know when it came to the history of rock and roll. His mind worked differently than most, categorizing information and sorting it into facts that he could regurgitate at will. I saw this as a challenge, always trying to stump Grant with musical trivia that he might not know, in hopes I could surprise him with something new. This came to be somewhat of a little game between us. He would greet me throughout the day with facts about music, although they were always poorly executed, inappropriate, and out of context. It was one of Grant's endearing qualities that was entertained by anyone who would listen. "Mr. Clark, did you know that The Clash's song called Rock the Casbah was written after Iran banned rock music?"

"I can honestly say I did not know that Grant, you got me again." I said, trying to avoid a patronizing tone. Of course, the facts Grant recited were something very few people knew, which made the behavior all the sweeter for Grant.

One day, however, after one of the many musical conversations between Grant and myself, I mystified him with a wonderful fact that he was delighted to know. From that point on, he began referring to his guitar as "Lucille," referencing blues musician BB King's famous relationship between singer and instrument. Grant paused his lesson to carefully lean the guitar down against his leg, the base of the guitar upright, now resembling more of a cello as it rested against his body. He bent down and reached under his chair for something. I heard a ruffling sound, saw a glimpse of a yellow plastic bag, as his hand fumbled through it and came back up with several potato chips.

"Really man?" I said, in playful disbelief. "You're not supposed to be eating those in class.

"Hey I'm hungry, I'm a growing boy."

"Fair enough, but let's keep this between us."

"No problem dude. Want one?"

"No, I don't like chips."

"You're weird."

Grant took the barbeque flavored chips and spread them out on his desk, ensuring that the chips didn't come into contact with one another. "I hate when they touch," he said purposefully. Grant picked up the chips, one at a time, savoring each piece, holding it just between his upper lip and his nose, inhaling, sniffing, and breathing in the aroma of the food, coated in salt and tantalizing flavors. But rather than place the chip in his mouth, he licked the open side of the chip, scraping off all ingredients, clearing it of any chance to retain its original flavor. He did so with visceral enthusiasm. Once satisfied with his sweep of the chip, he rotated it over, and repeated the process on the opposite side.

The other students were starting to take notice of Grant's behavior, wrinkling their noses in disgust, making repulsive faces, and talking under their breath. The discordant sound of guitars drowned out their jeers and teases, my stomach turned a little watching Grant toy with his food. "So is that how you eat your chips?" I asked leadingly. I knew Grant wouldn't pick up the sarcasm in my voice and would take me literally, failing to note the implication of the question. Grant's diagnosis of autism left him challenged when it comes to accurately reading facial expressions and detecting when a joke is on him.

"Yes this is the way." He urged carefully, with tedious precision.

I wanted to help, "Can you not just put them in your mouth and chew them up and swallow, without the pre-chewing ritual?"

"Oh I don't ever eat them!" Responded Grant, unabashedly. "I don't eat crunchy foods."

"I see..." I said questionably. "In that case, you're going to need to pack those chips away and finish them later."

259

Grant looked confused, and hesitated. "I'm not about to give these chips up, they're too tasty!" I looked around again and the other students were only getting more worked up with each passing second. I knew that another 20 seconds could mean that one of them was going to say something rude and belittle Grant in front of the class. This was one of those times when Grant was bringing the ridicule on to himself, not doing himself any favors to make friends. "Put the chips away or you are going to grease up your guitar and it will be ruined," I said firmly. A light bulb went off in Grant' head, as if that possibility was a horrible outcome to contend with. He relinquished his hold on the chips and returned them to their hiding spot under his chair.

"I may never eat chips again," he said, seemingly enlightened. Not wanting to embarrass him further, I said, "We'll talk about this later." With the chips out of sight and Grant's reputation still salvageable at the moment, I decided it was time to change the subject. "Scoop up that guitar and see what you can do."

Eddie called out from across the room, "Why doesn't my guitar sound good, Mr. Clark, I'm doing everything right aren't I?"

"Well yes but a guitar is supposed to have six strings, that one you're playing only has four." Eddie would go on to smile carelessly and continue aggressively plucking the strings. Before he could say anything else, Grant interrupted, "So what do you think was behind this song, "Comfortably numb?" Like, what's it all about dude?"

"Ummm, I don't know," I said, unconvincingly. Not wanting to go down a Pink Floyd rabbit hole. "Maybe we can talk about it in a few years."

"Want to know what I think? I think the band Pink Floyd was on a huge acid trip and that's what the song is about. It's like they're lost and numb from drugs, but totally comfortable!" Grant said, as he guffawed hysterically at himself, clapping his hands in celebration. Pleased with himself, it sounded as if he had personal experience with the roots of the famous song.

I chuckled, watching Grant become self-satisfied, "You may be on to something there."

"It would be so epic, to be a rock star, you know?" He lay back in his chair with his guitar and kicked his sandals off. Grant committed one social blunder after another. "You gotta leave your sandals on dude."

"Don't you want to smell my feet?" he laughed. "Just kidding, I'll put them back on."

Unlike the majority of students, Grant came from an affluent family, his father was a doctor, his mother a lawyer. Grant had moved from the southern part of the state. He could easily function in a less restrictive environment, had it not been for the unfortunate decision he made a year prior. Grant was previously placed in a private school where he was caught with a pocket knife and expelled. This offense haunted him and landed him at Bishop. But in a true testament to his character, only several months had passed and Grant had already met criteria to transition back to a mainstream school. When we would talk about the knife incident, he always insisted he never had malicious intent regarding the weapon, and I believed him. The knife, he swore, was a birthday gift and he simply wanted to show his friends. It was one of those very same friends who turned him in to the principal. Whereas most kids his age would feel double-crossed, surprisingly, Grant didn't hold a grudge against his friend who reported on him, despite the other students' sentiments on the matter, who would tell Grant that his friend was a snitch and he should seek retribution. After some time and consideration, Grant came to the conclusion that he made an irresponsible choice, broke the rules, and was paying for the consequences.

Despite his progress at Bishop and outstanding academic performance, I always got the feeling he was misunderstood by his parents. This was largely evident in school meetings, when teaching staff would brag about how wonderful and polite he was, yet his parents would default to snobbish, disdainful remarks, "Yea, well we wish he would just be normal. Why doesn't he just go outside and make friends? He hardly understands any sarcasm, we can't go anywhere in public without him embarrassing us." On paper, Grant's parents had a professions that more than qualified them to understand that an autism diagnosis for their son didn't make him less of a person. His parents, however, wanted perfection. They wanted someone with profound intelligence and perseverance who would become an upstanding, contributing citizen of the community and carry on their highly reputable legacy in the world of business. What they got instead, was a child who was different than most kids his age--awkward, quirky, low drive to become rich and powerful, still intelligent, but simply put, a goofball. His parents saw these characteristics as personality flaws.

Grant was one of those rare kids who was incredibly precocious for his age. He landed somewhere on the high end of the autism spectrum, of which one of the defining characteristics is the inability to navigate social situations and establish meaningful relationships with others. It was this characteristic, perhaps, that protected him from having his heart broken by the person who turned him in. Notwithstanding his past indiscretions, he still had an abstract idea of friendship. Although only needing one hand to count his true companions, he remained jovial, never allowing his feelings to get in the way of a good time. He was a companion and a great conversationalist.

"So I heard Trey went off, man. I saw Deputy Richards put him in the back of his police car and drive away for the day. What was that about?"

"Not really appropriate for me to talk about. Let's just say he made some bad choices."

"Figures. Had a feeling Trey was going to do something wild today."

"Yea?" My ears perked up. "What makes you say that?"

"Something he said to me this morning. Said he was planning to go off."

Grant's comment suddenly aroused my suspicion.

"Are you telling me Trey planned on getting arrested?" I asked speculatively.

"Well, he said he didn't want to go home, something about how his dad was back in town. His parents split, and I don't think he likes his dad very much anymore."

"Interesting," I said. "So, did he ever mention why he feels that way about his dad?"

"Ummm, kind of," he responded. Grant had a worried look on his face as if he had said too much. "I don't think I should say anything else," he said reticently.

If one were to describe Grant, shyness isn't a word that would come to mind. His uncharacteristic diffidence affirmed I was on to something important. Briefly, I felt that I had enough information, but after reconsideration, I decided to pry further.

"I respect that you don't want to do anything that may hurt Trey. But really, the more information I have, the more I may be able to help him, and possibly prevent something bad from happening."

"I guess I understand that..." Grant sighed and gave his next move some thought. "Okay, I'll tell you a little more, but you didn't hear this from me." My curiosity was peaked and I silently nodded in agreement.

"All I really know is that Trey casually mentioned something about how when his dad is home, he doesn't see his mom around the house very much. He said he saw her locked in her room one time, naked, curled up in a ball, with her hands tied to the dresser. And when he tries to go in there, his dad kicks him out and tells him he's not the man of the house yet. Then…after his dad leaves town again, his mom still stays in her room for several days at a time, and never comes out."

"Trey said all this to you?" I said as I studied his face, trying to read his hesitant emotion.

"Yea man, or wait, maybe that's not quite right. There was something else about how he saw her one time, but her face was half covered with a towel." Grant started rushing his words together, faster and faster as if to signal he was growing more uncomfortable.

"Something about her having the towel and trying to cover her face, but Trey saw a big bruise on her face anyways. His mom said she slipped on the wet floor and that's how she got hurt, but he was pretty sure his dad was responsible. He asked his dad about it and was told to mind his own business. Something like that," he said nervously. "I don't know, I'm getting all jumbled up now," Grant finished uncomfortably. He shifted in his seat uneasily.

"Sure man that's fine. I won't ask you anything else, that's plenty of information." I said assuredly. I patted Grant on the shoulder compassionately to comfort him. "Alright, let's take a shot at this song again, whattaya say? We're going to make you a rock star." Grant quickly returned to his normal, jovial self and the conversation was soon forgotten.

"Let's take it from the top, make sure your fingers are correct, and don't strike the strings as hard, it's not an aggressive song." Grant laughed and stood up out of his chair, he took a wide stance, flipped his mop hair down in front of his face and began playing a series of unrecognizable notes as if he was in front of thousands of fans who were cheering his name. He received uproarious applause from his peers, even I caught myself joining in on the fun, clapping and dancing. All the while I couldn't help but think of Trey who was at the forefront of my mind again. I had known Trey was methodical, but this...this took some considerable planning and foresight. The outburst, the computers, the arrest, all a part of his grand scheme to avoid his abusive father. For him, going to jail and spending the night in a cold jail cell is better than going home. The implications were heavy. There I found myself, feeling a sweep of sorrow for Trey Not holding a grudge, just wondering if he would be okay when he returned home. *I would need to escalate this report to Deputy Richards and let law enforcement take it from there. People don't just snap. It's the contributing variables in someone's life that influence their choices. Trey seized an opportunity to escape an abusive home, role play the dangerous fantasies that accompany his disorder, and act out on his rage. It's no wonder he has become what he has become. His decisions don't make sense to most people, but they make perfect sense to Trey. Maybe, if I had the power and took away one, or two, or three of these unfortunate events that qualified Trey's behavior, he wouldn't have acted out today, maybe he wouldn't be at Bishop, and maybe he would be a happier teenager. The more we pull away the curtain, the more details of a person's life that become unveiled, the easier it becomes to find out what motivates them to behave the way they do. Perhaps we should all dig a little deeper before judging others.*

It was conflicting moments like these that I remember most from Bishop, these small instances in time that left me utterly polarized. Unresolved, I advocated the cheerfulness in the room by clapping and smiling while Grant continued on in rock star fashion. Meanwhile my heart quietly grew heavy, celebrating for Grant's rare approval from his peers, and mourning for Trey in the same moment. I was comfortably numb.

Chapter 11

Dismissal

Three obnoxiously noisy yellow buses pulled through the entryway of campus and lined up in front of the school office. I was smacked in the face by the sultry exhaust fumes. Insulted by the smell yet again, I held my breath and tucked my face in my shirt. It was 3:05 pm, almost time to punch the clock. The cranky bus drivers barked orders at the gathered staff as if they were drill sergeants and we were new recruits entering boot camp. No matter how kind we were to them, we were met with pointed fingers and indignant looks, particularly when students' behavior resulted in their bus route getting delayed. At least once a day, there was a purposefully defiant student who decided to run off campus specifically to avoid going home, for any number of reasons. Generally, I empathized with the bus drivers' impatience. They had a job to do; sadly, I could never quite convince them that I was on their side. Collectively, anyone involved in the dismissal process felt immense pressure to round up all the students; after all, hadn't we earned our rest too? Approximately 90 percent of the time a departing bus was followed by a sigh of relief from myself and my comrades, signifying another day's work done. Time to go commiserate and lick our wounds. Casual conversations would take place on better methods to handle messy situations should they occur again. On occasion, however, a fight would erupt on the bus and it would turn back around, prolonging everyone's silent celebration and prompting us to negotiate our preconceived tolerance to stress.

The bell rang and the students poured out of the classrooms, high-fiving one another in celebration, eager to go home and watch television or play video games. There was much commotion as staff and students said their goodbyes for the day, casual conversations spoken loudly over the bus engines. One by one, the students took their seats and buses departed. With each bus that pulled away the staff's breathing became easier, as it signaled respite for everyone. But it wouldn't be that easy after all.

Mr. Williams's familiar voice would find itself over the air for the final minutes that day, "We are missing one student on the last bus, we have a headcount of 14 when there should be 15!" He fired away.

Trevor.

Trevor was particularly fond of inconveniencing everyone at his discretion. An unsuccessful adventure trying to smuggle lizards, beetles, or centipedes in his pockets meant he would surely stymie the bus departure. "This is an all call for the last bus. Has anyone seen Trevor? If he doesn't show up in the next two minutes he is going to miss his bus. Someone will have to sit with him for a few hours until his mom can get off work and come get him."

That sounds like a raw deal, I said to myself.

I glanced around at the group of staff, all looked pessimistic on Trevor's whereabouts and hoped for a miracle. We all shared a common thought, we needed this day to be over. The closest person in proximity to me was Mrs. Jones, appearing almost catatonic. I couldn't discern if she heard the call, her face was stoic. Not much had changed since our conversation earlier. Her forlorn expression still carried the face of a woman oppressed by her own heart, betrayed by how her good intentions to fix everyone had failed her. She had returned to looking utterly hopeless.

"We need Trevor now!" Mr. Williams said, blasting my ear drums. "Has anyone seen Trevor? Somebody find him now! His bus is taking off!"

Trying to overcome the disruptive humming of the buses, I scrunched my nose and wafted my hands to move the air along as the bus exhaust lay foul in the atmosphere as it had done earlier in the morning. I was sick of being yelled at through my ear piece. Frustrated, I ripped it off and slung the wire over my shoulder. "Mrs. Jones" I said, doubtfully, "Have you seen Trevor?"

There was a slight tilt of her head towards the sound of my muffled voice drowned out by the idle buses, a muted acknowledgement that I had addressed her. She made hesitant eye contact with me before shaking her head left and right to indicate "no" as her answer. Disappointed, I scanned the campus, several adults stood nearby calling Trevor's name. *This has been one hell of a day, I'd like to end it here,* I thought. *Where could he have gone?*

Trevor's bus driver was especially cantankerous and subject to ill-tempered behavior. The same driver that met me each morning with her ever-positive attitude. She curled her lip as if to say she was disgusted with me. Poking her head out the window, she spat her tobacco on the concrete and it made a spattering noise as it landed some feet below. She locked condescending eyes with me as if I was personally to blame for her route getting delayed. She spoke aggressively with a tone of interrogation, "You seen that boy?"

I felt like being a smart ass. "I saw him earlier," I said dryly.

She laid it on thick, "Ain't got time for this shit today," she said with a smug face. "I can't be late or my supervisor is gonna rip me up. Imma tell him its yall's fault out here."

I wanted to explain to her the gauntlet I had been through the preceding six hours and possibly evoke some sympathy. *Try being covered in grits, slapped in the face, running approximately five miles in cheap dress shoes, dodging rocks large enough to split your head, being spit on, hit, kicked, punched, and receiving death threats-- then by all means, take your frustration out on me.*

Begrudgingly, I said, "Gimmie a minute or two, I'll track him down."

With the tobacco lingering on her lip, she rolled her eyes, pulled the lever inside the bus, closed the door, let her foot off the brake, and began to drive away. *No cooperation.*

"Just stand by for one minute," I pleaded with her through the bus window, tossing my hands in the air, irritatingly. "I might know where he is."

"STOP THE BUS!" I heard a child yell, but unsure of the direction it was coming from. "STOP THE BUS PLEASE!" I heard again.

The bus squealed to a halt.

I desperately looked around trying to locate the voice. Just on the outskirts of campus beyond the tree line, I saw flashes of blue, grass stained jeans and oversized white tennis shoes between the trees. Chewbacca emerged from the bushes as Trevor had fully committed to his alter ego. Underneath the Star Wars mask, surely Trevor wore an expression of exhilaration as he was likely grinning from ear to ear. I half expected a pack of storm troopers to follow closely behind while Trevor dodged shots from their laser guns. Clearly an intergalactic battle was taking place that I was not invited to. A perfectly justifiable reason to hold up the bus departure in his mind. Trevor emerged from the trees covered in dirt. He ran clumsily, barely able to endure the weight of his red and blue backpack that clapped on his back, weighing twice as much as he did. He sported decorative Star Wars key rings that rang like bells as they hung from the straps. He cupped his hands together protecting something valuable. By all appearances this mysterious item in his hands was irreplaceable. Just before the grass met the asphalt, Trevor pathetically attempted to jump a heavy log, the weight of his backpack suppressing his effort to move yet again. His foot got hung up on a branch and he face-planted in the dirt, his backpack now shifted atop his head. Trevor was

277

slightly stunned with the wind knocked out of him; yet inexplicably, he hadn't relinquished his hold on whatever it was he carried. With a Chewbacca face full of dirt and his hands still clasped together, he used his elbows to support himself, found his legs, and raised himself to his feet with wobbly knees, just as a boxer would who had been knocked down and stood up for one more round of war. What would normally have discouraged him only seemed to motivate him now. He was eyeing Mrs. Jones, electrified as he sprinted towards her.

"Mrs. Jones! Mrs. Jones!"

Trevor found himself passing the bus in the middle of the road, meeting the bus driver's eyes, prompting her jaw to drop in disbelief that Trevor's current intergalactic mission trumped her schedule. The driver's arms swung wildly in the air as she stuck her head out the window and castigated him, "Have you lost your damn mind boy?" (Splat). She fired another round of tobacco at the concrete. Trevor ignored her and continued decisively towards his target. Mrs. Jones, still in her trance, was shaken abruptly by Trevor's body weight as he smacked into her side nearly toppling her over. Turning to look at him with a lukewarm facial expression, she grew impatient. "What is it Trevor?" she said hopelessly. "You nearly knocked me over. You need to get on your bus."

Trevor removed the mask and had the look of someone who had been berated, but managed to rebound quickly. He took a deep breath, still holding his hands clasped together. Excitedly, he looked up at her with his ocean blue eyes and said, "Well, I'm real sorry about being late for my bus and all. But when I went to find you in your office earlier to talk about how my lizard died and how sad I was, I noticed your flowers were in your trash can. So guess what? I ran out into the woods and I got you this because you deserve better."

Trevor raised his arms towards Mrs. Jones' face. He slowly unclasped his hands revealing a wild blue iris flower that shone radiantly under the warmth of the sun. Its flashy blue petals were perfectly shaped and pointed, giving way to an emerging bold yellow and translucent white where all three colors intersected. By all appearances Mrs. Jones had been plucked out of her somewhat catatonic state. Just then a slow smile crept upon her lips before lighting up her face like a Christmas tree.

She hunched over to lower herself to Trevor's height, unsure how to respond but still smiling exuberantly as her dark hair fell down into Trevor's face and tickled his cheeks.

"I wanted to find something very special for you!" he remarked. "Is it special enough?"

"I think it is incredibly special...How did you know this flower would mean so much to me?" she said. Trevor inhaled and stole the air from around him to build up an answer.

"This flower is special because I found it in the woods by itself, where all the other flowers around it aren't growing for some reason. Ya know what I think that means? I guess that means that you gotta try to find the sun if you want to grow. And when it rains, you get wet, but like this flower you just grow from bad times, too. I think that's what I learned here at Bishop."

Beckoning for Mrs. Jones to take the flower from him, Trevor followed up, "Well go on, take it silly."

"Well kind sir, how deeply insightful. I must say I am pleasantly astounded. You don't know how much this means to me," she said appreciatively.

Imagine that.

And for the first time in a while, I saw a spark of Mrs. Jones returning to her former, genial self. *She's going to be just fine,* I thought.

Just then the bus driver's voice echoed through the air, "Trevor, get your damn ass on this bus!"

Trevor carried his grin towards the bus, not knowing how truly touched Mrs. Jones was by his defiant act of kindness. He leapt onto the bus steps, and the door sealed behind him. The sun cut through the trees overhead and beamed off the bus, splitting the bus windows into some partially shaded and unshaded areas. The silhouette of Trevor's cumbersome backpack could be seen through the windows of the bus as he found his way towards the back and plopped down in a seat. Though the students rarely thanked the staff, we felt their appreciation in small doses each day as they hung their heads out the bus windows and waved goodbye to the hard working adults that lined up outside to see them off.

Eddie hung his head out the window, still publicizing his breakfast that morning with syrup on his chin matched by a goofy smile, both his hands raised in the air as he danced to his own internal music and swayed side to side in an arrhythmic motion. The window behind him showed Zahra, her hand waving a polite and ceremonial farewell, the gesture beguiling for her age, as her opposite hand guided her thumb to her mouth, signaling her continued juxtaposition and disharmony between adulthood and adolescence. The bus continued moving forward and Jacob stuck his head out behind Zahra, waving a peace sign with his pointer finger and middle finger, "Sorry about those grits, Mr. Clark!" he shouted. I nodded my head up and down and held out my hands loosely, indicating I had moved on, and let a smile on my face, permitting him to feel relieved as well. Behind him Zack and Cole wrestled one another and fought for headspace in the window, neither of them winning. Duncan's red hair appeared as he quickly popped his head out the window, just long enough to shout, "Get that damn internet fixed by tomorrow!" with enough conviction to have me slightly worried, before dipping his head back inside the bus and returning to his own world. Lastly, a Chewbacca mask reemerged from the bus for one last encore, from the very last window available. Underneath it, Trevor waved goodbye assiduously and pretended to shoot lasers from his fingers.

I mused at the hilarious, and somewhat normal way with which the day was brought to a close. The image of the bus driving away, kids laughing, the staff outside, carrying on informal conversations, teasing one another, the unforgivable exhaust emanating from the buses. At first glance, one would never think these students were anything but normal.

"That is something to be said for Bishop," I heard Mr. Morales's voice close by, as if he was reading my thoughts. I had not talked to him since my close call with Trey. He shuffled his black hair and powered off his walkie-talkie for the day, I followed suit. He seemed slightly fatigued from putting out fires with many of the other students, diffusing his own sets of crises while I was sharing my musical talents in guitar class.

283

"What's that, you say?"

"Well it's just funny how these days end, like nothing abnormal ever happened," he suggested. The bus was out of sight now, just a small dot down the road from what the eye could see. The smoke and dust had begun to whirl around and ascend from the immediate air, making it a little easier to inhale.

"I was just thinking that, but then again, what happens here is *normal* here," I said to him.

Mr. Morales lightly tensed, as if he wanted to make a point, so I let him express himself uninterrupted. "Well yes, agreed, what is normal at Bishop isn't really normal anywhere else. But still, look at what these kids go through on a daily basis. You and I go home to a sense of stability." His hands were moving in small circles, emphasizing his point. "As for the kids, on the other hand, we have no idea how truly difficult their home situations are, we can only speculate based on what we see and hear." I nodded my head, endorsing what he was saying.

"But the fact that the kids go home happier than when they showed up is worth something, makes you feel like you are making a difference. It's a miracle. Despite each day that carries its own events rattled with turmoil, the inner turbulence within each student, and their frenzied, volatile behavior, these kids still leave school with a smile on their face."

To that I added, "Not because they prefer missing school, but because they were given the chance to show up."

From his switchboard, Mr. Williams chimed in over the intercom speakers that were attached to each building on campus, playing disc jockey, his baritone voice slowly echoed throughout the school grounds, "This next one's for Mrs. Jones," he said, using his gift for gab and carrying his voice over theatrically for dramatic effect. "Me and Mrs. Jones" played over the speakers. Mrs. Jones paraded her blue flower through the air with her hand raised high, singing her theme song, and the staff joined in collectively.

Chapter 12

Transcend

It had been three years since I left Bishop. My own business was beginning to slowly but surely pick up some traction. The population of kids I worked with now were much different. Many of them young children, equally in need of intervention but far less plagued by abuse, neglect, poverty, gang influences, or exploitation. They come into my office well groomed, with clean clothes, and live seemingly healthy lifestyles with adequate care from their parents. I continue to derive practical solutions from those gritty experiences I was a part of at Bishop. Not all of my ideas translate, because of the drastic change in setting, geography, and population. But I am never able to forget about the kids I met at Bishop. During moments of silence I find myself pondering their whereabouts, asking myself, *What happened to them?*

In life, there are constant reminders of pain, sorrow, or happiness. Such reminders are sprinkled in our environment and tease us as we move through our day, provoking a memory or a passing thought, begging us to fantasize about past decisions and the outcome of those choices had we acted differently. For me, something special happens when I walk through a convenient store. My anticipation of a seemingly mundane task will be betrayed by moments of nostalgia. I'll pull the black rectangular-shaped handle to the building's glass door to open it wide, then take several quick strides inside as I always find myself in a hurry, even when I'm on time. I'll greet the woman at the cash register in her blue collared shirt and jeans. She will ask me how my day is, I'll be polite and automatic, telling tell her It is "just fine." I will move in close to her and tell her, "I'd like a coffee and $20 on pump 5," then place a $50 bill in her hand, just like the $50 bill Chad pulled from his sock. She will wave her hands in the air and complain about the cash register not working properly before thumping it several times with an open hand to force its cooperation. As her hands move before my face and she produces change from my bill, I will catch a lingering scent of cigarette smoke that disagrees with me. I will look at her disheveled hair and silently wonder if she has just rolled out of bed. She will ask me, "Want any candy to go wit yer coffee?" Her voice will remind me of the bus driver's voice that used to yell at me, but I am relieved because she is wearing a smile and seems much nicer. "We got some candy on sale to your right." I'll glance to my right, and tell her, "I'm not a big fan." But then, amongst the multicolored vast array of dazzling, iridescent sugar filled options, a brown wrapper will catch my eye. It will have bold, confident blue words across the front supported by a white backdrop and red border that outlines the word written on the plastic. The word that runs across the candy bar will say "Snickers." *Chad,* I'll say to myself. Something in my head, a stubborn voice, will tell me I want the candy bar, even if it is an uncharacteristic purchase for me. Reluctantly, I'll tell her, "Yea, throw this Snickers bar in there as well, please." She will ask me if I want a bag, and I'll politely decline, because it seems unnecessary. I'll thank the attendant, pour myself a coffee in a convenient store "to go cup," and then I will leave.

I'll begin the drive several blocks over to my office. My phone will ring, and an old friend will call me with an update on a former Bishop student. He will tell me Chad's been arrested for grand theft, and is looking at time behind bars. When I get to my office, I'll fight the urge to run inside. I'll force myself to take my time getting out of my car. There are no fights breaking out inside my office, there are no irate parents publicly abusing children, there are no police officers on standby, no crackling of tasers, no children running through the street, there simply is no crisis.

Instead, what waits for me inside my office are numerous e-mails that need my attention, voicemails that need to be checked, quarterly reports, insurance quotes, and unfinished patient evaluations that require finalizing. Later in the day, my clients will come in, and they will cry, scream, hit, and tantrum, but it will not be like Bishop. I'll walk inside and I'll sit at my desk, the time will read 8:55am. My eyes will scan the front door over the white font that reads "business hours 9:00am-6:00pm." *Five minutes until we open*, I'll say to myself. Instead of relishing the solitude, I'll start itching for something drastic to do. I'll start thinking to myself, *Doesn't someone need me? Somewhere, there must be a crisis that I need to respond to.* But there isn't. It will just be me, my coffee, and my Snickers bar. I'll look around my stack of documents and data sheets, until I locate my mug that says, "Behavior counts," in red italicized font. I'll slowly pour the coffee out, transferring it from the convenient store cup to the mug that defines me. I'll open the Snickers bar, note the syrup oozing alongside the wrapper. I'll laugh at the curiousness and peculiarity of my breakfast. Slowly, I'll take several bites, chew, and swallow, before chasing it down with my coffee, which I have plenty of time to drink now. When I get halfway through the candy bar, I'll stop... I'll listen to the sound of absolute silence, and take several deep breaths. I'll wrestle with the ambiguous feelings that come with not being needed immediately. I will feel both useless and relieved. I'll wrap up the remaining candy bar in what's left of its wrapper. And then I will tell myself, "I'll save the rest for Chad," whenever I see him again. Who knows, maybe I'm a misfit too?

Epilogue

It took me several years to become conscious of how Bishop has affected me. The more experience I gained in my professional field, the more my thoughts and decisions reflected on Bishop as my "home base." When I find myself wrapped up and consumed by stress in my work life, I can let my mind travel back in time, pretend I'm one of those students, touch "home base," and remind myself that my situation could always be worse, rendering me thankful for what I have. Therapy, schools, special education, teachers, communities, people, happiness, health, mother, father, abuse, money, trauma, depression, love, hate, rage, "normal." The deeper I get in the world of behavior health, the more I come to acknowledge that "normal" is relative and everything is seemingly intertwined. What if we stopped trying to make unique individuals "normal?" What if we embraced what makes people different, and allowed those unique personalities to shape our culture? As a behavior analyst, I don't have the luxury of believing in luck, not professionally nor personally. What I do believe in, is cause and effect. In life, we are all motivated differently. While I can't speak for everyone, the effects of creating actionable strategies that influence lasting change on someone's life simply outweighs the monetary or emotional value that can be collected by other means. Perhaps that is why I've settled in my profession. The "cause" of people's problems are variable, but the "effects" of receiving help can be enduring. The best treatment for all our problems is simply people helping people.

Success is variable, and I'm certain all students achieved a degree of success at Bishop they may not have accomplished elsewhere. When you are a professional working with such a population, the odds are already stacked against both you and the individual needing treatment. For the preceding story to be useful to the reader, it was imperative that I draw from experiences that most accurately represent how abuse and trauma manifests itself when intensified by behavior disorders. I have shared these experiences with the reader not to impose shock value, but to accurately represent the overlooked societal struggles that are facing generations of our children and adolescents. I'll be the first to admit

Bishop was not perfect, but much like behavior, it was evolving. Behaviors such as cursing, fighting, noncompliance, and self-injury, were an everyday occurrence. And while they did not always occur at the magnitude of each chapter depicted in this story, such situations required the care and expertise of a behavior analyst and other specialists with similar backgrounds in order to effectively respond to a child's needs. As mentioned in the beginning of this book, there are people with expertise who are capable of handling such problems, but are currently being denied access to public schools across the nation; forced to sit on the sidelines while students are left untreated by school systems and community programs that are failing America's youth.

I would like to underscore the following point: I have outlined dysfunctions that occurred on a micro level, specific to the student highlighted in any given chapter. Such dysfunction does not stem from a program that is failing the child, but rather stems from genetic predispositions, or environmental conditions such as psychological, physical, emotional, or sexual abuse having impacted the child's life negatively. The students portrayed in this story are going to exhibit dysfunction regardless of where they are or who is around them. Notwithstanding, the overall system at Bishop was a well-oiled machine that worked on a macro level, allowing some students to graduate high school with degrees either from Bishop, or from a mainstream school after they were repopulated back into a typical education program. I cannot profess my admiration for the teachers at Bishop enough. They always found ways to reach their students, and were successful in spite of the insurmountable odds that they were faced with daily. Each student at Bishop knew that they could come to a place where, in spite of what was going on in the world around them, they would be treated fairly, and given a real chance at an education in a supportive, nurturing atmosphere. This is what teaching should be.

Some students at Bishop performed very well academically, their curriculum required little to no tweaking from that of a typical mainstream program, illustrating that had it not been for his or her behavior disorder, academic performance would not be susceptible to deterioration. Thankfully, Bishop was there to support the student's needs such that they could rehabilitate themselves and accomplish their goals. Other students struggled with academics due to their below average intelligence, qualifying them as intellectually disabled and learning disabled. Interference from behavior and mental related conditions such as anxiety, obsessive compulsions, or autism, also contributed to their uphill battle. In these cases, curriculum was adjusted and behavior programs were modified to fit their needs, allowing them to be successful in their own way. I've found that individualized success differs greatly from the general public's idea of success, and is incongruent with the attitude and beliefs set forth by mainstream expectations.

Though Bishop was lenient in areas where other schools were not, it still had its limitations in which disciplinary action was necessary. In the interest of honest and transparent disclosure, current public school and national center for education statistics reveals Bishop's out-of-school suspension rate falls at 60.6% during the year

2013-2015, with school-related arrests at 5.6%. However, it is illuminating to report that its expulsion rate for these same years is 0%, effectively emphasizing its rehabilitative mindset. Also worth mention, is that throughout the years 2013-2015, Bishop graduated 50% of its eligible students, while 95% of its students had learning disabilities; in contrast to the median percentage of learning disabled students in the same state, at 23%. In comparison, the graduation rate for eligible students within the respective district ranged between 77%-87%, in a district that receives approximately 10,000 dollars in revenue per student. For a point of reference, 5% of the Bishop School students were enrolled in AP courses, with 83% of the population being male and 17% female.

My question to the reader is, why haven't we established more schools and programs such as Bishop? Keeping in mind that many students with hardened behavior disorders are repetitively expelled from schools, forcing families to pack their bags, move to a new city, and continue a pattern dead set on repeating itself. Why not give children opportunities to show us their strengths instead of their weaknesses? For one to understand the importance of this program, one has to understand the history of the students that attend the school. Children do not choose their parents, but oftentimes pay for their parents' decisions. My exposure to Bishop was the first time I was introduced to students who came from generational poverty, chronic uncleanliness, and multiple forms of longstanding abuse. After becoming witness to events at Bishop, I was convinced that poverty, (although obviously not found in the diagnostic and statistical manual of mental disorders), can almost function as a disease in its own right. In the beginning of the book, several variables impacting reliability of treatment and recovery were discussed. When you have a child who comes from an impoverished community, has a diagnosable mental or behavior disorder, and additional afflictions that exacerbate (or may be the cause of) his disability, such as instability within the family, physical, sexual, emotional abuse or neglect, trauma, limited access to resources, lack of training by caregivers or teachers, and a community that distrusts and misunderstands that which is different, more often than not the result is an individual who becomes a community burden. The ability to access funds and resources for treatment-related support is largely enfeebled by all of these confounding variables.

Without a program such as Bishop, there is the likelihood that such students would have been unnecessarily placed in even more restrictive programs governed by the state, such as state institutional psychiatric placement programs, correctional institutions that use punishment procedures with little oversight, or even worse. According to analysis by the Bureau of Justice Statistics, in the year 2014, for every 100,000 persons aged 10-17, 3000 of these children have an arrest record resulting from violent crimes and property crimes, such as murder, rape, robbery, burglary, arson, motor vehicle theft, and vandalism, to name a few, (as cited in OJJDP, 2015).

Because of the nature of an individual's intellectual disability, this leaves them with impaired cognitive processing capabilities, and deficient adaptive behaviors most of us use for logical reasoning. Subsequently, these individuals are subjected to victimization at alarming rates. Astoundingly, revealing and informative research by Davis (2009) supports that such people with intellectual disabilities "have a 4 to 10 times higher risk of becoming victims of crime when compared to those without disabilities" (as cited in Sobsey, 1994, How do people with intellectual disability get involved section, para 1). Furthermore, Davis asserts that "children with any type of disability are 3.4 times more likely to be abused compared to children without disabilities," (as referenced in Sullivan & Knutson, 2000, How do people with intellectual disability get involved section, para 1). Stories about victimized children were prominent within the student population at Bishop, many of them subjugated by those they were born to trust. As nauseating and revolting as it is, I have tried to rehabilitate disabled adults in group homes who fell victim to sexual and physical abuse from their direct caregivers who were hired to take care of these disabled people, but rather chose them as easy targets to commit despicable acts and violate them instead. Such individuals often have IQ's lower than 70 (average IQ ranges from 84-114), suggesting they are unable to process, much less communicate, these traumatic events to someone in a position to help. Unfortunately, this vulnerability makes them easy targets for potential abusers.

Conversely, such individuals with disabilities can more easily find themselves becoming perpetrators of a crime. Because they may not fully comprehend or rationalize the consequences of their actions, they may yearn for acceptance, and are easily manipulated into gang-related activity and criminal behavior to gain respect or be led into false friendships. An intellectual disability also inhibits that person's ability to communicate, leaving them more susceptible to arrest from a police officer who misunderstands them, exploitation from a trusted friend or caregiver, and longer incarceration times and diminished chances of parole, which may be a consequence of their inability to understand or acclimate to the culture of prison life. For these reasons, many students at Bishop succumbed to gang life. It is heartbreaking to report that several of the students whom I came to work with and know very well, were shot and killed while involved in gang related activity. Not because Bishop failed them, but because the community failed them.

Chad was a prominent character in this book, so much so that he earned more than one chapter. He is a perfect example of someone with an intellectual disability, who is cognitively aware that he is disadvantaged, yet vehemently protects his reputation and self-esteem by trying to disguise his disability. He does so by repeatedly making choices that he does not fully grasp and pretends to understand social situations but fails to truly do so. He has difficulty expressing himself, while finding superficial explanations to rationalize his delinquent behavior; is easily influenced; and is therefore easily targeted for manipulation. In other words, to keep his disability from being uncovered, he is someone who will nod his head to his peers and go along with a bad idea rather than admit he has no clue what is happening around him.

Elsewhere, Davis indicates that "those with intellectual disability comprise 2% to 3% of the general population, they represent 4% to 10% of the prison population, with an even greater number of those in juvenile facilities and in jails," (as cited in Petersilia, 2000, How do people with a disability get involved section, para 2). This type of character personality contributes to a substantial makeup of prisoners. Davis asserts that within prison populations in the United States, "4.2% of inmates have mental retardation," (now labeled intellectual disability) (as indicated in Veneziano & Veneziano, 1996 How do people with disability get involved section, para 2). An exhaustive report completed by a statistician by the name of E. Ann Carson, states that in the year 2013, there were "1,574,700 persons in state and federal prisons, an increase of approximately 4300 prisoners (0.3%) from 2012," (Carson, 2014, para 1). If previous studies referenced are remotely stable, then 4.2%, or approximately 66,137, of these incarcerated individuals had an intellectual disability of some kind. Of course tracking down the personal and educational history of each one of these individuals appears to be too tall an order to accomplish. However, one can't help but begin to imagine how many intellectually disabled prisoners themselves were products of poverty or perpetual abuse since childhood, and what may have become of them had they been offered better parenting strategies or a rehabilitative way out?

Not surprisingly, research points to intellectual disability as a high risk factor for homelessness. Economic hardships befall intellectually disabled (ID) individuals because they are vulnerable, have limited access to care, a lack of education, a history of abuse, a lack of employment assistance, possible exposure to drugs, and may not have developed a job trade that can be long lasting. For those out there who still consider these issues as weightless or insignificant, consider that in 2015, an analysis found that, "As many as 73,000 Texans with intellectual disabilities are on a waiting list to receive home-and community-based services, such as employment assistance, behavioral counseling, dental care and placement in small group homes with around-the-clock caregivers." (Savage, 2015, para 8). These are individuals living on the streets or in homeless shelters with no help. Across the United States, "Lakin et al (2010) estimated that nationally 122,870 persons with ID/D were waiting for residential services in 2009," (Bonardi et al 2011). This study further concludes that "The 2010 Annual Homeless Assessment Report to Congress (HUD, 2010) reported that 3.3% of all adults in permanent supportive housing, a support offered as a means to end homelessness, were identified as having a developmental disability, which would largely include those with an intellectual disability." (Bonardi et al 2011). Lastly, Lakin et al (2010) reports that roughly 37% of the homeless population has a disability of some kind. (Bonardi et al 2011). As a reference point for Bishop School, 55.9% of students were eligible for free lunch, which meant their families were at or below 130% of the poverty level.

In short, what do individuals with disabilities have to look forward to? How are we as a society shaping their future? The aforementioned research suggests that they are at higher risk of ending up homeless, in prison, or becoming criminals. As a population, we must stop sweeping these problems under the rug. We have to absolve ourselves of the idea that children with special needs are unteachable, and that they are somebody else's problem. Famed political activist, Noam Chomsky, once said, ""If you assume that there is no hope, you guarantee that there will be no hope. If you assume that there is an instinct for freedom, that there are opportunities to change things, then there is a possibility that you can contribute to making a better world."

Consider taking a look at Dr. Temple Grandin. As a child, she didn't speak until she was 4 years old, she was treated poorly by her peers and got in many fights, while her community rejected her. She wore strange clothes, had verbal tics, and talked funny. She is now arguably the most popular person in the world with autism, an accomplished author, public speaker, and a leading expert in animal behavior, among other things. She has also changed the entire landscape of agriculture with her work in safe and humane cattle handling. You never know when someone may surprise you.

To this day, there is a lack of mainstream knowledge when it comes to children with special needs, such as autism, intellectual disabilities, or emotional behavior disorders, because there exists a fear and callousness of what we don't understand. Bishop is a school that uses positive behavior support programs to treat and rehabilitate behavior illness, allowing individuals to become more independent, while giving them opportunities to express themselves, and most of all,

learn what appears to be a lost art in this day and age--
effective communication. As illustrated, some students
have benefitted greatly from having Bishop in their lives,
and have gone on to write their own stories for success.
Problems outlined in this story are not isolated issues.
These are community if not global issues that are
affecting the world as we know it. We elect leaders that
we trust to make decisions for the greater good. Where
do the funds for these children go when they disappear
into thin air? Funds that could aid in rehabilitating these
students, making them contributing members of society,
preventing unnecessary incarcerations. Where is the
political leader, on a local, state, and national level, that
will acknowledge the growing need for rehabilitative
programs that will keep America's children safe? Where
is the politician that does not act on his own free will,
representing his own personal goals? Those in office are
intended to represent the people and the opinion of the
public. Society has it backwards, the people follow a
politician, when the politician should follow the people.
Only by increasing public knowledge and awareness, can
those in a position to make a change turn their heads to

the sound of a parent's cry for help. When the interest of the public changes, so too will the interest of our elected leaders. As a whole, I challenge our educators, our political leaders, our mental and behavior health workers, our parents, and anyone else in a position to make a change, to start thinking outside the box when it comes to educating our children with special needs. In spite of the challenges I encountered at Bishop, I don't reflect on it with a heavy heart. It was a place not far from home, where I learned that an ounce of prevention is certainly worth a pound of cure. After all, the only way to surpass the world's expectations for our children is to set those expectations ourselves.

References

Bonardi, A., Lauer, E., Mitra, M., Bershadsky, J., Taub, S., Noblett, C., (2011) Expanding Surveillance of Adults with Intellectual Disability in the US. Center for Developmental Disabilities Evaluation and Research (CDDER), E.K. Shrive Center University of Massachusetts Medical School.

Carson A. E. (2014) *Prisoners in 2013.* Bureau of Justice Statistics. Retrieved from https://www.bjs.gov/content/pub/pdf/p13.pdf

Center for Disease Control (2015). Treatment. Retrieved from http://www.cdc.gov/ncbddd/autism/treatment.html

Center for Disease Control (2016). Data and Statistics. Retrieved from http://www.cdc.gov/ncbddd/autism/data.html

Davis, L. A. (2009) *People with Intellectual Disability in the Criminal Justice System: Victims & Suspects.*

Retrieved from http://www.thearc.org/what-we-do/resources/fact-sheets/criminal-justice

Jeffrey, T. P. (2014). *DC Schools: $29,349 Per Pupil, 83% Not Proficient in Reading*. Retrieved from http://www.cnsnews.com/commentary/terence-p-jeffrey/dc-schools-29349-pupil-83-not-proficient-reading

OJJDP (2015) *Law Enforcement & Juvenile Crime*. Statistical Briefing Book. Retrieved from http://www.ojjdp.gov/ojstatbb/crime/JAR_Display.asp?ID=qa05200

Savage, J. (2015). Observer. *The Waiting Game*. Retrieved from https://www.texasobserver.org/texas-intellectual-disabilities-homeless/

The U.S. is Tied. Teachnology. Retrieved from http://www.teach-nology.com/edleadership/funding_for_schools/

United States Surgeon General (1998). Mental health: A report of the Surgeon General. Washington, DC: Author. Retrieved from http://www.asatonline.org/for-parents/learn-more-about-specific-treatments/applied-behavior-analysis-aba/

CPSIA information can be obtained
at www.ICGtesting.com
Printed in the USA
LVOW08s1037190517
535146LV00001B/36/P

Brandon Clark, a Board Certified Behavior Analyst, discovered his professional purpose during a journey down the road less traveled: rehabilitation of children with behavior disorders. Clark artfully tackles the problems faced by children with special needs, highlighting the uphill battles these individuals face with America's education system and how society treats those with disabilities, all the while challenging the reader to take a closer look under the surface of behavior disorders. Clark leads the reader on a high speed chase, raising important questions all too often ignored. In doing so, he becomes a strong voice for the unsung heroes: the parents, educators, social workers, and mental and behavior health professionals who encounter these unique children in their lives. This is a collection of his first hand experiences with emotionally disturbed children. It's an enthralling account of the wildest events, the heartbreaking realities, the hilarious moments, and the tragic and true. His story spotlights one of America's most unrecognized problems -- the disabled youth. This is a must read for anyone who comes in contact with the afflicted and disadvantaged.

Brandon Clark
Behavior Analyst

Progressi**V**e Behavior
Consulting LLC

ISBN 978-0-692-85441-9
90000

9 780692 854419